Curious

KING'S
CROSS

Also available:

Curious Kentish Town by Martin Plaut and Andrew Whitehead

Curious Camden Town by Martin Plaut and Andrew Whitehead

Forthcoming:

Curious Golders Green by Alan Dein

Curious

KING'S CROSS

Andrew Whitehead

Five Leaves Publications

UNISON

HOUSMANS

London King's Cross
St Pancras International

London King's Cross St.
Underground

London Euston

THE WATER RATS THEATRE BAR

1
2
3
4
5
6
7
8
9
10
11
12
13
14
15
16
17
18
19
20
21
22
23
24
25
26
27
28

CONTENTS

INTRODUCTION

Over the past twenty years, King's Cross has been through a more complete makeover than any other part of central London. The creation of St Pancras International, the extension of King's Cross Station, the development of the former goods yards, the majesty and vitality of Granary Square, the rediscovery of the Regent's Canal — it's been quite a rebirth. And with it has come the banishment of the sleaze which had troubled the 'Cross' — as locals call the area — for decades.

Any regeneration exercise on this scale is never going to be everybody's liking. The old sense of community has been disturbed; some redeemable residential buildings have been lost; and the newly-fashionable neighbourhood is not to everyone's taste. But the new King's Cross is smarter and safer than the old. And most of the architectural gems, including warehouses every bit as grand as Wapping's, have been saved. Some of the more iconic aspects of the old King's Cross, a quartet of Victorian gasholders in particular, have been transplanted to a new location, and a new purpose, on the other side of the canal. It may be unfashionable to say so, but both Camden Council and the developers deserve credit for the transformation.

At the heart of this endeavour has been sixty-seven acres of what was a brown-field site, the 'railway lands', which are now among the hottest corporate addresses in London. More than a third of that area is open space. Along with King's Place and the Regent Quarter just across the borough boundary in Islington, this is quite a revolt into style for an area which for generations had been defiantly unstylish.

Ever since the Great Northern Railway received Parliamentary approval in the mid-1840s to build its London terminal at King's Cross, the railways have shaped and defined the district. They brought vitality and a measure of prosperity to the area, while also causing the clearing of vast tracts of land and the resultant overcrowding and immiseration of the surrounding area. As so often with mainline stations, King's Cross

7

acted as a magnet to the transient and vulnerable. By the late nineteenth century, some of the nearby streets were red light areas — a reputation that lasted for more than a century.

The twin stations of King's Cross and St Pancras, so close that they share a tube station, opened in successive decades. St Pancras is the younger station but the older place name. It has given its name to not one but two parishes, as well as a vestry (George Bernard Shaw was an elected member) succeeded by St Pancras Borough Council '(Barbara Castle, later a left-wing Labour cabinet minister, and V.K. Krishna Menon, the main force behind the pro-independence India League, were at times on the council) which eventually became part of the London Borough of Camden in the mid-1960s. The name is still reflected in the Parliamentary constituency of Holborn and St Pancras. And while St Pancras Station may for many years have been in the shadow of its slightly older sibling, the birth of St Pancras International has given it a good claim to primacy.

King's Cross, by contrast, has never had a parish which took its name; there has never been a King's Cross vestry, or borough council or Parliamentary constituency. A Camden Council ward bears the name — but bafflingly, it doesn't include the station nor indeed anything north of Euston Road and stretches deep into parts of Bloomsbury which may not be entirely comfortable with the connection. King's Cross has endured an almost complete administrative anonymity. Yet somehow, the name has always shone more brightly. St Pancras is next to King's Cross, not the other way round.

There has been a cost to the cleaning up of King's Cross and its commercial (and, some would say, residential) gentrification. The advent of Google and YouTube offices has entailed the banishment of the queer, quirky and rebellious. Once it was precisely the marginal nature of King's Cross which offered space for communities which might have been seen as transgressive: a grand old gin palace became a rallying point for gay culture and protest; a vast coal shed hosted one of London's biggest rave venues; a once fashionable wood-panelled pub for travellers survived as a down-at-heel strip bar. Now, the gay pub is a smart wine bar — the rave site is an up-market retail and leisure complex — and the strip joint has been reborn as an award-winning real ale pub.

But at least these buildings have survived. King's Cross has avoided the slash-and-burn which has disgraced far too much urban regeneration. And there are other survivals which both surprise and delight: the astonishing ceramic lunettes based on scenes from fairy tales which still decorate sturdy mansion blocks in Somers Town; the enchanting Keystone Crescent with its pronounced, neighbourly, curve; the great survivor of London radicalism, Housmans bookshop, still at the south end of Caledonian Road where it has promoted peace and social justice for sixty years.

This isn't a history of King's Cross; it doesn't attempt to chronicle the courageous local campaigns to tame and humanise the ambitions of planners and developers; nor does it seek to include all the most important, splendid or renowned of local buildings. It is a celebration of the more curious, remarkable and insurgent aspect of these streets; an idiosyncratic selection of locations and the stories attached to them. The stations are here — though we have focussed on the public art which has come in the wake of their modernisation. The transformation of the railway lands is addressed, but more for the traces of the past it has accommodated than for the showier new buildings. And there is an unapologetic emphasis on protest and resistance, on the vernacular more than the elite.

There's something here for those familiar with King's Cross, those exploring anew and those who are simply curious. And we've a map to help you get your bearings. You don't have to put on your walking shoes to enjoy this book, but if it doesn't pull you to experiencing these streets for yourself, or seeing a familiar friend from a new angle, then we have failed.

1 | The King of King's Cross

King's Cross has been reborn more than once. The recent regeneration of the area is eye-catching in its scale and ambition. But almost two hundred years ago, the naming of the area as King's Cross was itself a rebranding of a corner of London which had become a synonym for dereliction and decay. And as part of this attempt to redeem the locality, there was briefly a statue of a king close to where the Lighthouse building now stands. So King's Cross really did once have a king at its principal crossroads — though without much in the way of majesty.

This corner of London was initially known as Battlebridge. It was the location of a bridge over the River Fleet and, rather more speculatively, the site of a battle which may or may not have involved Queen Boudicca and her followers. The name survives in Battlebridge Basin at the back of King's Place (home to the *Guardian*), which dates from the early 1820s, though the name is more recent.

Battlebridge did not have a lot going for it with its vast ash and cinder heaps (supposedly sold to the Russians to help with rebuilding after the Napoleonic wars), a huge mound of horse bones, a smallpox hospital and a few pockets of dilapidated housing. It was also notoriously prone to flooding and the reputed haunt of thieves and vagabonds.

The name was so sullied that it was a blight on the development of the area. The story is told in the most magisterial of Victorian-era local histories of London, W.J. Pinks's *History of Clerkenwell*, a parish which abutted King's Cross (there are still plaques on Keystone Crescent which show where the parish boundary once ran). Pinks records that developers of residential streets at the top end of Gray's Inn Road were determined to escape the malign reputation of Battlebridge. He cites the account of a grandson of William Forrester Bray, the man who came up with the solution:

> ...in consequence of the notorious popularity of the name
> of Battle-bridge, the new buildings would not let. The

REMOVAL OF KING'S CROSS.

result of this was that my grandfather had an interview
with the other freeholders to enable them to change the
name to a better one. One wanted the new built locality to
be called 'St. George's-cross.' Another wanted its name to
be 'Boadicea's-cross,' in memory of that great battle from

whence it derived its name. But neither of these names being agreed on, and my grandfather being the largest builder there, he proposed that, in honour of George IV, who had just assumed the crown [in 1820], it should be called 'King's-cross.' This was at once agreed to; all leases were granted under that name, and from that period the locality has made great progress in civilisation and improvement.

The first reference to King's Cross by that name in *The Times* — as good an indicator as there can be of an area's coming of age — appeared in 1830.

There was another impulse towards honouring the king in a new name for the area. A Neapolitan musician and music teacher, Gesualdo Lanza, managed to attract the patronage of George IV for quite the daftest idea King's Cross has ever endured. (Make that one of the daftest: there was a 1930s plan for a King's Cross airport with elevated runways, both radial and circular, to be built on top of the railway sidings — I wonder why that never got off the ground!) The Royal Panarmonion — with a name like that you can tell it's a touch dubious — was intended to be pleasure gardens, concert venue, baths, hotel... what you might call today a leisure complex. All of this was to be built where Argyle Square now stands. Some of it was constructed, including the theatre, but most of those associated with the scheme went bankrupt, and by 1832 the project had failed, and much of what had been put up was pulled down.

The architect on this ill-starred project was a local man, Stephen Geary. He also had another none-too-brilliant idea — that of building a splendid statue of George IV at the intersection of what are now Gray's Inn, Pentonville and Euston Roads. The king's crossroads!

But the king died in the summer of 1830 before the scheme had made much progress. And as he wasn't the most popular of monarchs, the money raised for the statue by public subscription was modest. Geary decided to press on but was forced to cut a few corners. An architectural journal republished — with silent but unmistakable scorn — a notice circulated as the edifice was being constructed:

> The Statue of George the Fourth, now erecting at King's Cross, is on a new plan; it is formed of bricks and mortar, by a working man. The finishing touches, however, bestowed by Mr. Geary the architect, have rendered it not inferior to stone, at least to the eyes of common spectators. The extraordinary cheapness of a figure thus got up is its great recommendation. The cost does not exceed £25.

Who did they think they were kidding?

Pinks, our parish historian, records that the 'colossal' eleven-foot high statue, completed in 1835, stood on top of a structure of octagonal shape fully sixty-five feet in height, replete with Doric columns. An 'architectural monstrosity,' he stormed, 'which grievously offended the eye of taste while it remained;' which wasn't long — the statue had an ever shorter span than the king's reign.

'The basement was for some time occupied as a police-station,' Pinks recorded, 'afterwards it became a public-house, when, to attract custom, a camera obscura was placed in the upper story. Previous to this latter change, however, the statue of the King was removed from its exalted station and broken to pieces, and the nose of the statue, composed of a draining tile, was offered to a learned antiquary for the modest sum of sixpence. In the year 1845, the entire structure was removed, and soon after a tall lamp was placed on its site.'

The Illustrated London News was relieved to report the removal within a few years of its construction of this structure which proclaimed to be King's Cross, a 'strange pile' topped out with what it called 'a very uncomplimentary effigy of majesty', so much so that it attracted the jeers and worse of cabmen and watermen. The king's cross was even less lamented than the monarch it commemorated.

So King's Cross, strictly speaking, disappeared from view fully seven years before the station that took its name opened for business.

Mr Geary, it must be said, had some successes in his architectural career. He was responsible for the first gin palace — though he later became an advocate of temperance. He also designed the magnificent Egyptian avenue and catacombs in the old part of Highgate cemetery — and that's where he is buried.

This renaming of the area almost two centuries ago worked — for a while. The coming of the railways once again mired the place in grime. As the area went down in social standing, overcrowding increased. King's Cross had — by the 1890s and perhaps earlier — become notorious for vice, a reputation that stuck until not that long ago. In the 1980s and '90s, King's Cross was synonymous with sleaze — drug dealers, street prostitution and rooms-by-the-hour hotels. The commercial developers of the railway lands are said to have considered proposing that the entire area be renamed to escape its reputation. Wisely, they decided against.

But a six-acre site immediately to the east of King's Cross Station and close to where the king's statue once stood has been smartened up and redesignated the Regent Quarter. The Prince Regent ruled while his father was too ill to attend to affairs of state, and eventually ascended the throne as — you've got it! — George IV.

2 | Hogwarts Express

London's most renowned rail station is celebrated around the world for a service which never makes it to the departure boards. It's even more elusive than the Virgin East Coast service to Edinburgh Waverley (remember that?). But the Hogwarts Express has been taking young wizards to their gothic boarding school — according to the more historically-minded Potter-ists — since shortly after King's Cross began operation as the London terminus of the Great Northern Railway.

Harry Potter and his mates boarded at platform nine and three-quarters, which for many years, muggles found a little difficult to locate. But when King's Cross emerged chrysalis-like from its much-needed makeover in 2012, the Hogwarts Express platform was there for all to see in the new and stunningly ambitious western concourse. Or to be more precise, what you could see was the push-bar end of a luggage trolley bearing cases and an owl-sized birdcage sticking out of a sheer brick wall with an appropriate platform sign.

It was an inspired design detail, and has brought more innocent joy to the world than the combined achievements of the top ten global architects.

Initially, passers-by could just pretend they were Hogwarts-bound and get a friend to take a snap. But as word got around, Potter fans descended

on the spot. In droves. Crowd barriers were put up, the nearby bookstore was reborn as a Harry Potter shop, and professional photographers were brought on board. It's now a cottage industry. The queue can take up to an hour. You can wear your choice of house scarves. And while you don't have to buy the professionally-taken photos, posing in mid-jump with the scarf flying off in Potteresque fashion — yes, there's a uniformed team to help you achieve that effect — is usually beyond the reach of a humble muggle pointing a mobile phone. The minimum charge for a 'proper' photo: £9.50. I make that about two galleons in wizarding currency.

J.K. Rowling, Harry Potter's creator, has recounted how her parents met on a Scotland-bound train from King's Cross. 'I never knew the slightest indecision about the location of the portal that would take Harry to Hogwarts, or the means of transport that would take him there.'

In the first of the series, *Harry Potter and the Philosopher's Stone* — which appeared way back in 1997, the year Tony Blair became Prime Minister — young Harry gets dropped off at King's Cross by Uncle Vernon: 'Well there you are, boy. Platform nine — platform ten. Your platform should be somewhere in the middle, but they don't seem to have built it yet, do they.' He's saved by Ronald Weasley's mum, who explains how it's done. 'All you have to do is walk straight at the barrier between platforms nine and ten. Don't stop and don't be scared you'll crash into it, that's very important. Best to do it at a bit of a run if you're nervous.'

Just to complicate the story, in the Harry Potter films the getting-through-the-brick-wall-onto-the-platform scenes are shot at King's Cross, but at a spot between platforms 4 and 5.

The day we stopped by at the Hogwarts platform, there were Australians, Mexicans, Japanese and Chinese patiently taking their place in the queue. It's the sort of attraction — a bit like the Tower of London

or Madame Tussaud's — that appeals much more to foreign tourists than to locals.

How do you feel — I asked one Potter enthusiast, as she divested herself of her Hufflepuff scarf — about standing in line for forty minutes to pay $12 for a single photo of yourself pushing a luggage trolley? 'Hey, I'm not likely to get another chance,' came the reply. 'This is the closest I am ever going to get to the Hogwarts Express. That's cool!'

3 | Entente Cordiale?

When Eurostar first linked London and Paris by rail in 1994, the train from the French capital pulled in at Waterloo. Difficult to believe, isn't it? For the first thirteen years of Eurostar, visitors from France disembarked at a station whose name celebrated Britain's most conclusive victory in battle against the French. Imagine how the Scots would have felt if King's Cross had been named Culloden.

In 2007, St Pancras International became the enduring home of London's cross-Channel rail services and the designers decided to commission a piece of public art which might banish the memory of Waterloo and offer some visual reassurance of the Entente Cordiale, the 'friendly understanding' which in 1904 represented a new start in Anglo-French relations.

The brief, says artist Paul Day, was that the sculpture should be 'romantic, democratic and as iconic as the Statue of Liberty'. He came up with a ten metre tall bronze of young lovers locked in an embrace — capturing, it's said, the romance of rail travel. It's situated on the Grand Terrace and although formally known as The Meeting Place — a misnomer, as it's tucked away from the busiest parts of the stations — it's inevitably become, in common parlance, the Lovers' Statue.

Day and his wife served as models in the initial designs for the artwork. In so doing, they gave a very personal edge to that old entente:

Day, who is British, lives near the French city of Dijon with his Anglo-French wife, Catherine. 'The statue is very loosely based on us but it was certainly in my mind that it could also represent that famous Entente between our nations and not simply a meeting of a man and a woman,' Day told us. 'I married a half-French, half-English girl whose father has become the first English member of the Académie Française so he is the embodiment of the Entente Cordiale himself. I have lived in France for twenty-five years. Our families really do live in the spirit of that Entente. Now my very French daughter has moved to the UK and so the cycle continues.'

Initially the couple were to be shown kissing, but that perhaps more Gallic rendition of the relationship, it was decided, was a bit too bold. 'My assistant took a series of photos of me and Catherine doing what came naturally,' Day has recalled. 'Catherine came up with the final pose, of the two foreheads touching and the woman's hand touching the man's face. It was much more poignant than a full-blown snog.'

The sculpture — reputed to have cost £1 million — got quite a kicking from artists and art critics alike: a 'terrible, schmaltzy, sentimental piece of kitsch,' according to Tim Marlow; 'a very good example of the crap out there,' snorted Antony Gormley; 'barely a work of art,' commented Jeremy Deller.

'Some will say it is a chocolate box sculpture,' Day responded. 'But I don't want it to be bound by the prevailing view of art. Meeting Place is an appeal to universal values.' Those who pass through St Pancras tend to be more generous to the sculpture than the fine art community — and are impressed as much as by its scale as the design or execution. It is a stonkingly big piece of art. But somehow twenty tonnes of bronze hasn't done as much for St Pancras as half a luggage trolley has pulled off for neighbouring King's Cross.

The Anglo-French lovers dwarf another statue on the terrace, of the whimsical and much loved poet and conservationist, Sir John Betjeman.

He is depicted looking up, gripping his hat to his head, with his paunch and waistcoat prominent, and carrying a canvas bag. The inattentive will immediately imagine they are at Paddington.

Betjeman railed and stormed against plans to demolish St Pancras and its 'exuberant Gothic' hotel, designed by George Gilbert Scott (the station opened in 1868 and the hotel followed five years later). It would, he warned, be 'criminal folly'. The statue — and a bar named after him on the Grand Terrace — are tributes to his successful campaigning zeal.

Although Betjeman grew up in and around Highgate, and is most remembered for his verse explorations of Metroland (the genteel suburban stops on the outer reaches of the Metropolitan line), his family was local to King's Cross. The Betjemanns (the second 'n' dropped away during the First World War) had a large cabinet-making workshop on Pentonville Road. The business specialised in dressing cases, decanter holders — the fancy, up-market, end of the trade. It's where the family's wealth came from.

'The smell of sawdust still brings back to me / The rambling workshops high on Pentonville', Betjeman reflected in his verse autobiography. But he resisted all his family's attempts to ensnare him in the business, which finally closed in 1945.

Betjeman was instrumental in securing Grade 1 listing for the station in 1967 but died in 1984, long before the resurrection of his beloved St Pancras. He would be relieved that the station's revival respects the original design and that the Midland is once more a hotel. As to how he might have regarded the bronze lovers towering over him, well, in The Olympic Girl he wrote: 'The sort of girl I like to see / Smiles down from her great height at me'.

So, wish fulfilled! Though Betjeman ends that poem on a more wistful note: 'Little, alas, to you I mean, / For I am bald and old and green.'

4 | Council Housing that Kills

Camden Town Hall, built in the late 1930s as the headquarters of the borough of St Pancras, was once a bastion of metropolitan radicalism. On May Day 1958, the Red Flag was flown here — one of the Labour councillors said he'd like to see it aloft above Buckingham Palace too. A generation later, the same building just south of Euston Road was the scene of one of the most humbling episodes for any Labour-run council — when its own tenants staged a month-long occupation of the council chamber and committee rooms in protest against unsafe council-funded bed-and-breakfast accommodation.

'There was an unimportant fire in the London borough of Camden on November 20. Nothing spectacular; just a cheap bed and breakfast establishment going up in flames.' Those were the opening words of a 1984 newspaper article by Salman Rushdie which focussed nationwide attention not simply on a fatal fire in overcrowded and inadequate council-funded housing — but on the landmark protest it provoked in one of London's (until then) less politically assertive communities.

Rushdie made a mistake in his opening sentence. 46 Gloucester Place — where the fire took hold, taking the lives of Shamim Karim, aged 27, her five-year-old son Nezamul and three-year-old daughter Shalaha— lies in the borough of Westminster. But they were Camden residents, out-housed for nine months in bed-and-breakfast accommodation beyond the borough's borders. The property was run by a company called London Lets and was being used — apparently without the knowledge of Westminster council — as a hostel for the homeless.

According to Rushdie, the fire extinguishers in the Gloucester Place building were empty... the fire alarm had been switched off... the fire exits were blocked... and the light socket on the stairs had no bulb in it. His article suggests that Camden councillors initially responded to concerns about the sub-standard housing by saying that it was in another borough and so not their responsibility.

'The family who died were among more than twenty people trapped after a rear staircase in the building collapsed,' the *Camden New Journal* reported. 'The bodies huddled in a third floor bedsit were found by firemen wearing breathing apparatus. Mrs Karim's husband was out at work at the time.'

One of those who lived there told the *Journal* that nineteen families — all Bengali — lived in the hostel. The breakfast that Camden council paid for was never provided. There were just two cookers in the building, and to make matters worse, Bengali families from neighbouring London Lets properties were also sent there to cook. Hot water and central heating were available for just two hours a day — one hour in the morning and one in the evening.

In the aftermath of the fire, some of the 700 families consigned by Camden to bed-and-breakfast accommodation came to a council meeting in Camden Town Hall. They wanted a proper inquiry into the fire deaths and the rehousing of all those in emergency bed-and-breakfast accommodation in council flats. When they were fobbed off, the families decided they were not going to give up without a fight.

They occupied the council chamber and corralled several councillors and officials — 'hostages' according to some accounts — until a platoon of twenty-five police officers pushed through the door and made a pathway through which the councillors left. The Labour councillor who called in the police was subsequently forced to resign as chair of Camden Council's 'race' committee.

The protestors stayed put in the council chamber and adjoining rooms for almost a month. 'Town halls are monuments to British stuffiness: the commissionaires, the panelling, the closed committee rooms,' the *Guardian* reported. 'So it comes as a shock to find in Camden's council chamber notices saying "No More Death Traps"; to see piles of mattresses in the corridors. And in the lobbies, large pans of curry. ...'

'About 20 of the families occupying Camden Town Hall are Bengalis; a racial minority in the capital, quiescent to the point of invisibility. The husbands — several are waiters or night cleaners — and their wives are awed by the municipal grandeur of the Town Hall. But they would be suffering still, in damp, cramped rooms, were it not for a fatal fire which, for this group at least, put an end to passivity.'

In London, of the four perennial urban concerns — health, housing, education and transport — housing has often been the most pressing political issue, especially in inner London where demand is highest and where poorer newcomers to the capital have tended to congregate. There is no escaping that migrants have often been allocated the worst, the most insanitary, the least safe housing — in part because the authorities expected that they would put up with it without too much complaint. The sit-in at Camden Town Hall was a clarion call that such awful and unjust assumptions were going to be fought. The occupiers became more determined when an initial investigation suggested that the fatal fire may have been an arson attack, giving rise to the possibility of a racist motive.

During the protest, a reporter from the *Journal* met up with Soowa Miah and his family — they previously lived in two small rooms in a hotel next to the one where the fire broke out and were camping out in the town hall's committee room three. 'They share it with several other homeless families, sleeping with his wife and four children on makeshift beds of mattresses and blankets. But Soowa says his present conditions are infinitely better than the one he has left behind. For the first time in eighteen months his family have space, heat, light and clean toilet facilities.'

Camden at first said it couldn't offer council housing to all those in bed-and-breakfast accommodation and it wouldn't allow those families occupying the town hall to jump the queue. The turning point came when the Labour leader of the council, Phil Turner, broke down in tears as he heard first-hand from the occupiers about their living conditions. That sign of compassion helped break the deadlock.

Eventually the council conceded that it would indeed endeavour to move all the homeless placed in temporary accommodation into council housing stock within two weeks. The occupiers refused to leave until they were convinced that the council would act on its pledge. As Christmas approached, Ken Livingstone —head of the Greater London Council — announced that he would visit the town hall 'to play Santa Claus and hand out gifts to children in the occupation'. The protest ended just a few days before Christmas, after the council announced further concessions.

Nasim Ali was a teenager at the time of the protest. He has spoken about bringing food to the families camped out in the town hall. He spent time in the council chamber doing his school homework and stayed there for a couple of nights. Twenty years later, he was back in the council chamber — as an elected member of the council. He went on to become Camden's first Muslim mayor. A few years ago, to mark the borough's fiftieth anniversary, Camden commissioned photographer Elly Clarke to take a portrait shot of Councillor Nasim Ali in the chamber he first entered during the housing occupation.

That's a sign of how much has changed, and for the better. But the Grenfell Tower outrage underlines how much has still to change. The headline on Salman Rushdie's article all those decades ago has a tragically contemporary ring to it: 'The council housing that kills'.

Mock Gothic meets mock noir! A toothy and deranged-looking Alec Guinness, in search of lodgings for his unlikely string quintet, stands framed by the door of his would-be landlady's house. Looming behind him is Scott's architectural masterpiece, St Pancras Station and Hotel. It's the most celebrated image from one of the most renowned of British movies. Much of *The Ladykillers* was filmed in and around King's Cross. Guinness's new lodgings — to judge from this shot — were straddling the road half way down Argyle Street. But then, appearances can be deceptive.

'King's Cross appears in many films — but there's no other King's Cross film,' comments the historian and broadcaster, Alan Dein. 'It feels like a documentary portrait of the area at a key point in its history, still with industry — railways, gas works — but an area decidedly going downhill. King's Cross comes across as a dark place.'

The Ladykillers is a soot-tinted comedy about the hapless gang who carry out an armed robbery at King's Cross and the old dear who unwittingly harbours them. Released in December 1955, it was the high-

watermark of the unsurpassable Ealing Comedies: ten or so films — movie buffs can't quite decide how many — which include such gems as *Whisky Galore*, *Kind Hearts and Coronets* and two other titles which reveal an intensely local London feel, *Passport to Pimlico* and *The Lavender Hill Mob*.

The key location is Mrs Wilberforce's subsidence-ridden house — so pronounced that the gang nickname her as Mrs Lopsided — backing on to the railway lines just north of King's Cross station. The opening shot sets the scene: wonky house, grimy Victorian mansion blocks lining the street and a steam train making its way towards King's Cross goods yards.

The house was a prop — assembled on location, capping the western end of what was Frederica Street (now gone, but close to the south-western extremity of Conistone Way). It's the best part of a mile away from Argyle Street and the view from the house's front door — but that's the movies for you. The production team faced a tricky problem, according to a *Daily Mirror* story from July 1955. They had spent £3,500 building the house with plywood, plaster and lots of paint — but Frederica Street was home to youngsters who were proud of their reputation as 'the toughest bunch in the neighbourhood'.

So, a deal was done (does this smell a little of film industry PR?): don't get in the way of the filming or damage the set, and afterwards there'll be a big street party. 'Yesterday the kids of Frederica-street had their party', the *Mirror* reported. 'One hundred and one of them ate all the cakes and ice cream they could hold while film stars waited on them.'

Photos have come to light of this unlikely *Ladykillers* Tea Party, with trestle tables in the middle of Frederica Street, kids guzzling pop, 'Mrs Wilberforce' joining in the fun, and members of the gang doling out the treats.

Katie Johnson, as Louisa Wilberforce, delivers the star performance of the film — a trusting but formidable woman harking back to an earlier era. She and her tea party friends (yes, there's one in the movie too) wear boater-shape hats decorated with artificial flowers, headwear of a sort

which — one suspects — had gone out of fashion before the First World War. Her late husband was a captain in the merchant marine who went down with his ship in the China Sea, but somehow managed to save a menagerie of parrots and cockatoos, one named General Gordon, who still provide company for Mrs W.

Alec Guinness plays the gently bonkers leader of the gang, Professor Marcus, who appears initially in shadow and silhouette, giving an air of menace to a comedy which has a higher body count than some Shakespearean tragedies. He hires rooms from Mrs W, and the rest of the gang — including Herbert Lom and Peter Sellers — pretend to be rehearsing musicians to give cover to their planning meetings. They can't play a note, of course, so the professor puts on a Boccherini minuet on a portable record player hidden in a battered suitcase... we hear quite a lot of it by the end of the film.

The truly superlative cast also includes Jack Warner (as a desk police officer, just the role he was making his own in *Dixon of Dock Green* which hit the TV screens in the same year), Kenneth Connor and a scene-stealing Frankie Howerd.

Argyle Street features in several of the shots — a corner of King's Cross which remains, architecturally at least, largely unchanged. Vernon Rise also figures prominently, offering a view down King's Cross Road to the station. That's the spot where the gang wait anxiously for word of whether the heist has worked and impatiently pile into a phone box when the crucial call comes.

The caper, a none-too-gentle armed hold-up of a lorry taking cases of bank notes to King's Cross Station, was filmed on Goods Way, Battle Bridge Road and Cheney Street, the then grimy cobbled streets which formed an arc round the north side of King's Cross Station. The gasholders that have been transplanted to the north of the canal and not so much gentrified as ennobled, loom over the spot giving a touch of grit to the action, and attentive viewers will also spot a block of Stanley Buildings and the German Gymnasium.

At the risk of spoiling the suspense, the gang succeeds in stealing £60,000 (the equivalent of about £1.5 million today) and in getting Mrs Wilberforce to pick up the trunk containing the spoils on the supposition that's she collecting some of the professor's luggage. But just as they are making good their getaway from Mrs W's, the muscle man, 'One Round', gets a strap of his cello case trapped in the door and in tugging it free, the case springs open and hundreds of bank notes fly out all over the street.

Mrs Wilberforce realises that the string quintet are robbers and determines to report them to the police. The gang try to put her off by insisting that she will be jailed as an accomplice, while drawing lots to decide which of them will kill her. None of them are up to the task, but they are all looking for ways of double-crossing their colleagues. One-by-one, as they fight and feud, they are consumed in steam and smoke from the trains and despatched off a railway bridge into coal wagons making their way in and out of the goods yards. Mrs W can't work out where they have gone — but when she goes to the local police station to explain all and ask them to come and collect the 'lolly', they assume that she's made it all up and tell her that the money is hers to keep.

The Ladykillers was re-released on DVD to mark the film's sixtieth anniversary. Alan Dein narrates a short feature on the locations captured in the movie. 'I must have seen *The Ladykillers* dozens of times,' he insists — 'and I still laugh in all the right places.' So will you!

6 | Prostitutes, the Priest and the Police

Of all the celebrated sit-ins, work-ins and occupations in and around King's Cross, the most renowned is at first glance the most unlikely — a twelve-day take-over of a local church by sex workers and their supporters. Holy Cross on Cromer Street declares itself 'the church in the heart of King's Cross'. None of the women occupiers worshipped there and whatever their grievances, they were not directed against the church or its minister. But Holy Cross was a one-minute stroll from the offices of a sex workers' collective, and not much further from what in the 1980s was the most notorious of London's red light areas, Argyle Square. So when activists sought to emulate the example of French sex workers, who had won a lot of attention through a series of church occupations, Holy Cross was the obvious choice.

It's an anonymous-looking brick-built church — without a tower, but with a pleasing if simple interior, and a very curious history. The first vicar persuaded the Church of England authorities to name the church in memory of his friend and relative, Commodore James Goodenough. He died of an infection occasioned by a poisoned arrow while poking around where he wasn't welcome in the Solomon Islands. The name of the island where he sustained the injury was Santa Cruz — hence the church of the Holy Cross. The bell from Goodenough's ship, the SS Pearl, was installed in the church where it continues to call the faithful to prayer.

From the start, Holy Cross — consecrated in 1888 — was firmly attached to the Anglo-Catholic wing within the Church of England. It

still is. Over the years, indeed, two of its vicars have been accepted into Roman Catholicism. The church was established to minister to the poor and marginalised community in the Cromer Street area, which even then had a reputation for sex work. 'This corner of London... is cursed by the street-walking form of prostitution,' the social investigator Charles Booth recorded in the 1890s, 'for which many of the small hotels in the neighbourhood of the railway terminal offer facilities.' Throughout its history, Holy Cross has had an impressive record of outreach among the homeless and refugees.

In the early 1980s, Argyle Square was often choked late at night by kerb crawlers trying to pick up sex workers who lined the pavement. Police tried to keep tabs on the pimps and drug dealers, as well as the women, and were not always gentle about the methods they used. The English Collective of Prostitutes was a group of radical feminists — not all current or former sex workers — which campaigned for a repeal of the laws that criminalised prostitutes and an end to racist and intolerant policing. They were then based at a women's centre on Torrington Street. Influenced by events across the Channel and unable to find any other way of attracting attention to their concerns, they resolved in November 1982 to occupy their local church.

'We entered in twos and threes towards the end of the church service, when we knew the doors would be open,' recalled Selma James, among the most prominent of the ECP activists. 'By the time the service was over there were about fifteen of us with sleeping bags and blankets sitting in the back. The priest came over to ask if something was wrong, and we told him we were staying overnight and why.'

The women had a list of demands — above all, an end to illegal arrests of prostitutes and the halting of police threats, blackmail, harassment and racism. They wanted prostitutes to be regarded as workers, not dismissed as vice girls. 'Mothers need Money', said the banner placed outside the church. As well as mats and bedding (some of the women remember that the church's stone floor was desperately cold) the women also bought fifty black party masks, so that they couldn't be identified in press photos and to ensure that prostitute and non-prostitute women would not be distinguishable from each other.

'I expected to be there for just one night,' says Nina Lopez who was breastfeeding her four-month-old son throughout the protest at Holy Cross. In the end, the occupation lasted for almost two weeks.

Every morning, the women ushered everyone else outside the church and had a meeting to make a collective decision on whether to stay another day, how to tackle the press and what leaflets to issue. They were above all out for publicity — they knew it wouldn't all be good publicity, but it would draw attention to their concerns.

Any journalist who turned up was directed first to the women's centre where their details were taken and their purpose ascertained and they then were personally accompanied to Holy Cross. The centre also monitored the press coverage and ensured that the occupiers knew what was being said about them.

There was a hand basin and toilet in the church, but nowhere to cook. A group of gay men brought hot food every day. Women from the peace camps at Greenham and Faslane came to show their support. The women's committees of both Camden Council and the Greater London Council were broadly on board. But the most memorable show of support was from the prominent Labour left-winger Tony

Benn and his wife Caroline, who turned up unannounced on Saturday evening.

'He said to us: "what can I do to help?"', recalls Nina Lopez. 'He didn't lecture us. They were respectful. They didn't have an attitude, like: oh, they're a bunch of whores.' Another of the occupiers, Sarah Walker, remembers her astonishment when Tony Benn got out his dictaphone and recorded a letter he would send to the Home Secretary and the head of the Metropolitan Police. 'He played it back to us, and we said "no, that's not quite right", so he re-recorded it. I'd never seen a politician doing anything like that.'

Benn referred to the visit in his renowned diaries. 'About forty women, of different nationalities and ages, some with babies, were occupying the church... They told us their grievances... They gave us tea and were photographed with us.' The ECP still has those photos of Caroline and Tony Benn amid the masked occupiers. When we met up with three of the veterans of that protest, they proudly pointed themselves out: Selma James is the woman with dark hair directly behind Caroline Benn; Nina Lopez is in the front on the far right with her baby on her lap; behind her in the checked dress is Sarah Walker.

At first, Father Trevor Richardson continued to hold services at Holy Cross, and the women made no attempt to stop the church being used for worship. But some of the regular congregation were fed-up of street prostitution and all the problems that went along with it. On the first Sunday of the occupation, 'Trev the Rev' debunked to a sports hall across the road. When he asked the congregation (swelled by reporters of course) to pray for the prostitutes, an elderly woman tried to shout him down.

'They have overstepped their welcome and I feel manipulated,' Father Richardson said of the occupiers. 'While I have some sympathy for some of the things the women are trying to achieve, I also have a great deal of sympathy for local residents who feel justifiably angry about the effects of prostitution in the area. I now wish to express solidarity with my parishioners, though not necessarily with their prejudices against prostitutes.'

The ECP gained a huge amount of attention, if rather less active support. And the occupiers wisely decided to come up with a demand which could easily be conceded — that the council appoint a monitor to keep an eye on what the police got up to in and around Argyle Square and to speak up for the prostitutes' welfare. A monitor was promptly appointed — a 'young brunette in bright green trousers' according to the tabloids, who followed her around on her first day — and having given the church a good clean and polish, the occupiers trooped out.

'I knew we had done something big,' says Selma James, who is now approaching ninety. 'We were all different people after those twelve days: we knew each other better, we loved each other. We learnt how to handle the press and how to work together. It was empowering.'

The women judge the occupation a landmark event: the birth of a more visible sex workers' movement. They argue that following the occupation, the media's approach changed — with less pejorative talk of vice girls. And police racism in particular was put under the spotlight. The council monitor worked less well, according to the ECP, because she wasn't accountable to the women and proved unwilling to take on the police.

Misgivings among local residents, however, were widespread. 'The ECP didn't have anything to do with local women and local prostitutes,' insists Linda Clarke, a feminist and left-wing activist who was secretary of the Cromer Street council tenants' organisation. 'It wasn't fun coming out of your front door and finding used condoms everywhere. And the protest just advertised this as an area for prostitutes.' She later helped to organise a local festival in Argyle Square with the aim of reclaiming for the community an open space which locals had come to regard as off-limits because of prostitution and drug use.

As for 'Trev the Rev', he denounced the departing occupiers for their 'bullying tactics'. Once they had left, 'We had a spontaneous celebration,' he recalled. 'About 25 people appeared. I carried back the Blessed

Sacrament, and we all sang: "Now thank we all our God".

The story of the occupation at Holy Cross has a curious codicil. The blaze of publicity surrounding the sit-in occurred as George Eugeniou was writing a play about the profound divisions in Cyprus, the land of his birth. Eugeniou is the founder and artistic director of Theatro Technis, which grew out of the Cypriot community in Camden and has for forty years been based in the Old St Pancras Church House on Crowndale Road. His play, *The Appellants*, was about a Cypriot couple — the man Greek, the woman Turkish — who were forced out of the island, but after several years living in London faced deportation from their new home. Drawing on events on Cromer Street, he depicted the couple and their young child claiming sanctuary in a central London church.

A couple of years later, George Eugeniou found his plot come to life on his doorstep. A Greek Cypriot refugee couple turned up. They had been given deportation papers; could he help? Remembering the play, he tried to find a church which would offer the couple a temporary home. The minister at St Mary's in Somers Town — also part of the Anglo-Catholic tradition within the Church of England, and once the church of the much admired Father Basil Jellicoe — agreed to provide a home for Vassilis and Katerina Nicola. They lived in the church hall for five months. There is no legal force to the claim of sanctuary in a place of worship — but with the support of the church and the local community, the couple were safe.

Eventually Katerina became ill and — after legal action and pleas to the home secretary had produced no result — the couple agreed to return to Cyprus. They moved in to a house vacated by Turkish Cypriots near Limassol. Eugeniou stayed in touch and a few years after the Nicolas' reluctant return to Cyprus they visited London as tourists and called in on their benefactors. It was, as Eugeniou says, a case of 'life imitating art imitating life'.

'The Hell-Holes of Hillview' — that was the story spread over three pages of the *Camden Journal* in October 1979. Talk about shitting in your own backyard! This sensationalist story in the local weekly damned one of the largest blocks of social housing in King's Cross to perdition and back.

Around 1890, the narrow alleys north of Cromer Street were demolished in an early slum clearance scheme. In their place, the East End Dwellings Company erected seven sturdy, four-storey mansion blocks intended for the industrious working classes. All were built around courtyards and had a mix of staircase and balcony access. At first, most flats shared a toilet on the landing; as late as the 1960s, for many residents a bath was a big metal tub kept in a cupboard.

Most of the blocks were built in the early 1890s, forming a sort of ladder with rungs stretching between Argyle Walk and Cromer Street. They fitted the novelist George Gissing's description of similar buildings on Farringdon Road: 'terrible barracks... sheer walls, unbroken even by an attempt at ornament.' That novel was entitled *The Nether World*, a reminder of the long history of likening this corner of London to hell. The last of the blocks, Tonbridge House — a measure more imposing — was completed in 1904.

Wind forward three-quarters of a century, and the model dwellings had sunk to the level of the slums they were built to supersede. They still felt Victorian: grim, austere, cramped and unmodernised. By the time Camden Council bought the buildings in 1974,

they had collectively been renamed — along with a few smaller, later, blocks, most directly fronting Cromer Street — as Hillview.

If you are wondering what hill these flats had a glimpse of, so too are the residents. Pentonville? Highgate? More prosaically, the estate is said to have taken the name of the agents who arranged its sale to the council.

The 1970s were a grim decade for Hillview. Camden Council started 'decanting' — moving out — established tenants, but lacked the resources either to refurbish the blocks or to redevelop the site. Pimps and drug dealers broke in to the vacant flats, adding to the miasma of dereliction and despair. Camden turned to short-life tenancies — and to a self-help organisation SCH, Short-Life Community Housing — to find ways of filling the flats with single tenants and so reclaim them from the drug dens and the brothels. It was a high risk strategy and took quite some time to deliver.

Camden also looked to SCH to take on another role — providing homes for evicted squatters. In August 1978, a large contingent of heavy-handed police officers broke up one of London's biggest — and most politicised — squats, at Huntley Street in north Bloomsbury. Ken Livingstone, then chair of Camden's housing committee, helped to secure new homes in Hillview for many of those thrown out into the street. The refugees from Huntley Street were used to life on the edge — but for many, Hillview was a frightening place. Street crime was rife, drugs users sometimes dossed in stairwells, the racist National Front was active and on occasions gun shots could be heard. And the death of Pat Malone, a sex worker living on Cromer Street — her body had been dismembered by an off-duty police officer — added to the sense of an estate beyond redemption.

It was just weeks after that tragedy that Angela Cobbinah, a reporter on the (you've guessed it!) *Camden Journal*, took up a short-term tenancy in Hillview's Whidborne House. She knew about the estate's terrible reputation but desperately needed a place to live. 'I was unprepared for the scene of utter disarray that sprang to my eyes when I opened the front door,' she wrote in her Hillview memoir, *From Hell Hole to Home*. 'Although the furniture had been removed, there was junk everywhere. Worse still, there were splashes of blood on the walls and discarded needles on the floor.' She was told the last tenant had died in the bath.

'It was like the Wild West — there was drug dealing everywhere, prostitution everywhere,' says Gary Fox, a former squatter who moved into Hillview at about this time. 'Council tenants wouldn't accept housing in that sort of condition, but we did because we did the work on the place ourselves.'

The angry 1979 issue of the *Camden Journal* that compared Hillview to hell carried an open letter on its front page addressed to Ken

Livingstone, whose office was just a two minute stroll away. 'Is it that you cannot see it or smell it from the air conditioned double glazed ivory tower that is the new £7.5 million Town Hall extension? Or are you looking the other way — in the vain hope that it will disappear.... It's the worst slum in the Borough, with conditions that belong to another century,' the paper stormed. 'PULL THE BLOODY LOT DOWN, WITHOUT DELAY.'

The reports by journalist Patrick Breen depicted a 'Dickensian' estate, where the old established tenants waited forever for simple repairs, while being overrun by noisy, anti-social, drug-using, short-life tenants and punk squatters. 'Hillview is like a bomb about to go off,' the *Journal* reported. 'The council tenants will wait ever-impatiently for rehousing. There'll be more attacks, more fights, more moans. The punks and mods will continue to take over empty flats... trying to sort out their muddled lives.'

As the paper noted, not everyone agreed with its anti-newcomer approach. John Mason — who had, the previous year, become Hillview's first short-life licensee — insisted that the punks and mods were not the cause of the problem but a symptom 'The blame has to lie with Camden Council,' Mason told the *Journal*. 'They have given up responsibility for the flats, leaving most of them empty — ripe for squatters... to move in.'

Four decades later, John Mason is still living in Hillview. He remembers the profound culture clash between the long-established residents, many of them widows and working class, and the new influx of youngsters who played music, loudly, all day and much of the night. The council tenants and the short-life residents were 'daggers drawn' according to Mason, and that's not simply a figure of speech.

Many of the squatters and short-life licensees brought with them, however, a track record of campaigning on housing issues and they injected new life and purpose into tenants' organisations. The combined campaigning of Short-Life Community Housing and the tenants' Save

Hillview Campaign — there was quite an overlap between the two organisations — shamed Camden Council into redeeming the estate. Lorna Whitehorn, who was brought up on Cromer Street and allocated a semi-derelict flat on Hillview, recalls that the action of the local Labour Party in deselecting two council grandees who were seen as letting down Hillview made a crucial difference. 'They learnt their lesson,' she says. And the new tenants learnt too — even managing to win Prince Charles over to their demand to smarten up Hillview not pull it down.

The short-life tenants worked hard to build bridges with long-established residents. SCH provided window boxes for all the flats; they arranged to power-hose some of the exterior to demonstrate that the blocks could be cleaned up; they put up sheds for the rubbish bins so that courtyards could be enjoyed in summer free of the stink of rotting refuse; they organised parties for local pensioners. At a time when Camden Council had abandoned giving housing priority for sons and daughters of tenants, SCH was able to give short-term homes to youngsters who would otherwise have been forced to live miles from their parents. They also took referrals from groups such as HIV charity the Terrence Higgins Trust and the African Refugees Housing Action Group — Ethiopians in particular have found a home in Hillview.

'We managed to clean up the estate and clear out the pimps and dealers,' Lorna Whitehorn recalls with pride. Some didn't go quietly; Whitehorn at one time had four sets of locks on the door of her Hillview flat. She helped organise the tenants' association and worked for SCH; she eventually led the negotiations with Camden about the future of the estate. 'I did the deal — a good deal,' she insists: Camden agreed that the estate would be refurbished rather than demolished; short-life tenants who had contributed so much to turning Hillview round would get an assured tenancy; and the blocks would be managed by a housing association.

It took seven years, starting in 1993, to transform Hillview, and the financial cost was high. This was a landmark for more than just the estate.

Serious money was being spent in improving the housing stock in one of London's most troubled localities. It showed that King's Cross could be redeemable.

The estate no longer seems grimy and those who live there no longer feel embattled. 'I wouldn't live anywhere else,' comments Gary Fox, who has lived here for almost forty years. 'I enjoy living here,' agrees John Mason. 'Hillview has settled down into a diverse but tolerant community. Short-life housing was full of oddballs; its long-term legacy is an estate where very different people live relatively harmoniously together.'

There's still concern about the 'g' word: gentrification. Much of the housing stock around King's Cross was built as, and largely remains as, social housing. With the new luxury blocks around Granary Square, the balance has started to change. A few of the Hillview flats are now being let at close to the market rent — which hardly any of the established tenants could contemplate paying. Some see that as an alarming sign of what may be to come.

But the estate, once the Hades of this part of the city, now has that attribute which in the 1970s seemed unimaginable: it's respectable.

8 | A Bug in the North Sea

If you like a good spook story, then this is really tasty. It's about the time that MI5 bugged a fish-and-chip shop.

Not just any chip shop, but the splendid family-run North Sea Fish Restaurant in Leigh Street, one of the better purveyors of this hallmark of British cuisine. It features in the tourists' guide books and deservedly so — as well as the lively take away, there's a smart sit-down area which does good business, more sizeable than the small frontage suggests.

It's well known that both the security service and the police kept leaders of the miners' union under close surveillance through the strikes of 1972 and 1974, which broadly the miners won, and the more turbulent dispute of 1984–5, which they lost catastrophically.

Mick McGahey was the best known of the Scottish miners' leaders and a prominent Communist. His phone was tapped by MI5, but — according to a historian of the security service — both his impermeable Scottish accent and the effects of his heroic appetite for hard drink made much of his conversation difficult to decipher.

Still, according Seumas Milne in his book *The Enemy Within: the secret war against the miners*, MI5 took the trouble to bug McGahey's regular London hotel, the County on Upper Woburn Place, where he stayed during meetings at the NUM's headquarters on Euston Road. (In 1988, with the NUM in steep decline, the union's HQ was moved to Sheffield, and subsequently to Barnsley.)

More than that, Milne records that the security service also planted bugs in the North Sea Fish Restaurant, where McGahey, union boss Arthur Scargill and other left-wingers on the NUM's executive used to

meet during the 1984–5 strike to discuss tactics. What they found out we don't really know: who went for cod, who stuck to the northern preference for haddock, and who couldn't resist the mushy peas? I guess we'll have to wait until the transcripts reach the National Archive at Kew... if they ever do.

The allegations were raised in the House of Commons by the left-wing Labour MP, Harry Cohen. So the establishment on Leigh Street must be just about unique among fish-and-chip shops in featuring in Hansard.

Seumas Milne, whose father was the BBC's Director General, was educated at Winchester and Balliol College, Oxford — so hardly surprising then that he ended up working on a journal called *Straight Left*, closely linked to a hardline faction in the old Communist Party of Great Britain. About the time the miners' strike began, Milne got a job on the *Guardian*, which is where he worked for the next thirty years. We wanted to check out what his sources were for the tale of the bug in the chip shop, but he's a little on the busy side, as Jeremy Corbyn's *eminence grise* (or to put it more formally, the Labour leader's executive director of strategy and communications).

Milne's book suggests that the information may have come from Cathy Massiter. She was a former MI5 officer who, in 1985, turned whistleblower and went public about her role and that of MI5 colleagues in the surveillance of the Campaign for Nuclear Disarmament, the National Council for Civil Liberties and left-led trade unions.

As for the restaurant's view on the bugging story, it's taken a leaf from the security service. Don't comment — don't even say 'no comment' — just keep mum.

9 | Father of Reform

The most splendid of the statues in our patch is that of Major John Cartwright, which has for approaching two centuries adorned the gardens that now bear his name. The inscription is quite as enthralling as the likeness — indeed even the typography, and the white-on-black design, takes us back to an earlier era.

Cartwright was a seafarer and military man who won the sobriquet of 'Father of Reform'. In 1776, the year we lost our colony across the water (more on that later), he wrote a book entitled *Take Your Choice*, one of the first publications to advocate thoroughgoing Parliamentary and franchise reform. He argued for four of the key demands taken up by the Chartists sixty years later: manhood suffrage, secret ballot, annual elections and equal electoral districts.

As well as making the case, Cartwright also campaigned for Reform — at first through the Society for Constitutional Information, and in his seventies as a leading member of the Hampden Clubs, platforms for radical political debate in the years after the Napoleonic wars.

And the statue? Well, this area was developed at just the time Hampden Clubs flourished, 1811–1817, and the crescent street to the west of the gardens took the name of its builder and developer, James Burton. More than thirty of his grand Regency houses still stand, many of them now small hotels. In 1820, Cartwright moved in to 37 Burton Crescent, and he died there four years later a few days short of his 84th birthday. His esteem was such that a bronze statue by George Clarke was commissioned, paid for by public subscription and erected in 1831. It's been there ever since, showing a seated Cartwright looking wisely and pensively towards the student halls of residence to the east.

The inscription celebrates not simply Cartwright's patriotism and his political radicalism, but also his championing of incipient American nationalism. 'He was the first English Writer who openly maintained the Independence of the United States of America;... he nobly refused to draw his Sword against the Rising Liberties of an oppressed and struggling People.'

He had, as early as 1774, published a pamphlet supportive of American independence... which entailed an abrupt end to his naval career. He

subsequently became a major in the Nottingham militia, the rank which he gloried in for the rest of his life.

But it was a full eighty years after Cartwright's death that the garden and the crescent were renamed to bear his name.

There's nothing Victorians liked as much as a gory unsolved murder. Burton Crescent delivered a double dose. In 1878, an elderly widow who ran a boarding house at no. 4, Rachel Samuel, was brutally killed in her own kitchen. Suspicion fell on her cleaning woman, but there was insufficient evidence to bring charges.

The popular press got into even more of a lather about another murder, at no. 12, six years later. The house seems to have been a brothel. Mary Ann Yates appears to have picked up a man on Euston Road and taken him back to her room. She was found the following day strangled. The killer was never traced, and given the nature of the murder it has attracted a lot of unseemly attention from Ripperologists.

The combined effect of these murders was that Burton Crescent became a sort of Rillington Place of its day. The lawyers, surgeons and writers who made up much of the local population petitioned the parish council for a change of name. But it was only in 1908 that both the street and the gardens were renamed after the major, or more particularly his statue, and became known as Cartwright Gardens.

Even then, the street couldn't escape a certain notoriety. In the 1920s, a Collins detective novel appeared with the sort of title that must have infuriated the denizens of this neighbourhood — *The Cartwright Gardens Murder*.

I wonder how our pioneering reformer would have felt about 'his' gardens being accessible only to keyholders. That persisted until as recently as December 2016 when, after the rebuilding of the students' halls on the east side and smartening up of the gardens and tennis courts, the whole area became a public space. It took a while, Major, but your gardens achieved democracy in the end!

10 | EGA Stays OK

'It was a wonderful campaign, an admirable campaign — incredibly well organised and very enjoyable,' says artist and writer Lynn MacRitchie. 'You met a fantastic range of people — people who believe in something.'

A long-running campaign too — and that rare beast, one that the campaigners won, well, after a fashion.

MacRitchie is looking back forty years to the struggle to save the Elizabeth Garrett Anderson hospital, one of only a handful that were for women, by women — so all those seeking treatment there knew they would be seeing a woman doctor or consultant. After five years of uncertainty and three years of vigorous campaigning, the EGA was given a reprieve and stayed on Euston Road — not forever, but for another twenty years or so.

For a year or two, MacRitchie spent just about every Monday evening at the EGA. The doctors, nurses and support staff staged a 'work-in' and occupied the hospital. Campaigners mustered, round-the-clock, a permanent picket to ensure that there was no out-of-hours attempt by the health authority to wind-down facilities.

Lynn MacRitchie's regular slot on the picket rota was Mondays starting at 6pm. She would come early and eat in the hospital canteen, and then spend the evening with the same two fellow campaigners — one a dockers' shop steward and the other a radical feminist. The 'Save the EGA' campaign brought together doctors and trade unionists, anti-cuts campaigners and women's groups, the old left and the new left. It also cut across the usual political fault lines: a Labour government sanctioned the hospital's closure and a Conservative government saved it.

Elizabeth Garrett Anderson had become, in 1865, the first woman to qualify in Britain to practice medicine (James Barry, assigned female gender at birth but living as a man, had qualified earlier but that hardly diminishes Garrett Anderson's pioneering status). Eight years later, she became the only woman member of the British Medical Association, which promptly changed its rules to bar any other women from joining.

The dispensary at which she worked became the New Hospital for Women, which in 1890 moved to purpose-built premises on Euston Road. Elizabeth Garrett Anderson died in 1917 and the following year the women's hospital was renamed as a tribute to her. In the 1970s, it had more than a hundred beds, operating theatres and a range of activities which extended well beyond gynaecology and obstetrics. But as far as the local bureaucracy of the NHS was concerned, it didn't quite fit — a small, stand-alone institution, many of whose patients came from beyond the local catchment area. The increasing Bangladeshi presence in the locality brought with it more demand for women patients to see women doctors, but that wasn't factored in to the decision making.

The first sign of impending crisis came when the General Nursing Council decided in 1974 not to send any more trainee nurses to the hospital. That was a body-blow for any teaching hospital. Barbara Castle — ironically the cabinet minister behind the Equal Pay Act — visited the EGA and announced a few months later that it couldn't survive on its Euston Road site. Staff became convinced that the health authority was running down the hospital. The lifts broke down and were declared too expensive to make good, which meant that the operating theatres could no longer be used. The EGA campaign must have been just about unique in highlighting the demand: 'Repair the Lift'.

The hospital staff set up an action committee, an at times uncomfortable alliance between doctors and consultants on the one hand

49

and on the other staff organised by the left-leaning National Union of Public Employees (NUPE). In November 1976, they decided to occupy the hospital. 'Pickets "guard" the door all day to ensure that there is no sudden attempt to move patients or equipment to another hospital,' the *Daily Telegraph* reported. 'They are understandably wary of the authorities, who closed down the hospital's maternity home in Belsize Park at an hour's notice.' Staff were working 'in almost impossible conditions' but daily clinics were continuing 'and patients are cared for before and after their operation in other hospitals in the three first-floor wards.'

Lynn MacRitchie lived nearby in a squat on Northington Street and then at Huntley Street but had never been referred to the EGA nor knew of it. She worked as a domestic assistant at the Royal Free Hospital in Hampstead where she was a NUPE shop steward, but she spent as much time as she could with the Poster Collective based at another local squat in Tolmers

Square. Through her involvement in the women's movement, in housing campaigns, as a trade unionist and as an activist artist, she was drawn to the EGA campaign, designing some of the posters and lapel stickers which were so effective in getting the message out: 'EGA Stays OK!'. She still has a copy of the 'Save the EGA' poster she designed.

A key success was the involvement of local tenants' groups — indeed

they were the bedrock of the movement. Linda Clarke was a council tenant on Cromer Street and working on a doctoral thesis about the development of Somers Town. She was also an anti-cuts activist. She became the lynchpin of the Save the EGA campaign. 'It was hard work. I spent bloody hours on it. I've still got the picket rotas somewhere. It was a time when there were lots of occupations — but I don't think anybody had tried to occupy a hospital.'

She says she learnt a lot. 'We had to combat that feeling that: oh well, it's all lost. It was an uphill struggle. We'd go to meetings with the health authority which were 95% depressing and 5% positive and we'd immediately go to the *Camden Journal* and tell them about the positive bit.' The EGA campaign linked in with other attempts to save hospitals from closure — activists recall visits to Hounslow and Plaistow, so that the strength of one campaign could inspire others.

It worked. Even the *Daily Telegraph* was obliged to declare that 'almost every women's organisation in the country has offered support'. So too did the only woman politician who matched Barbara Castle in charisma and profile. Margaret Thatcher declared that she was 'a staunch supporter' of the hospital. Within days of the Conservatives' election victory in May 1979, the new government announced that the EGA would be upgraded on its Euston Road site. £2 million was to be spent on providing a forty-bed gynaecological unit and eighteen day care beds. This wasn't the sizeable general hospital for women that the campaigners had sought — but it was a victory. 'Yes, I felt elated,' MacRitchie recalls. 'We all snorted that it was a Tory government that reprieved it. But we wanted a hospital for women to be kept open, and it was. And if we hadn't campaigned, it would have closed for sure.'

The EGA kept going until 2000. Its name survives in a wing of nearby University College Hospital. The Euston Road building, which once faced demolition, is still standing — and in one of those wonderful quirks of history, it's now the national HQ of the trade union UNISON, a direct successor of NUPE.

The entrance hall of the old hospital and an adjoining room are now a small memorial to Elizabeth Garrett Anderson and the institution that took her name. It's worth popping in, though not many do — the displays and decor are well intentioned but a touch sepulchral. 'I don't think a lot of people are aware it's there,' laments Linda Clarke, now a professor at Westminster Business School. 'A lot of UNISON people aren't even aware it's there!'

Of course, what the 'Save the EGA' campaigners wanted was a hospital for women not a memorial to it. So there's a bitter-sweet aspect to it: a reminder of a protest that prevailed — but a cause that was eventually lost.

11 | The Fairy Tale Estate

It's not what you might call obvious fairy tale territory. Somers Town has a reputation as a rough, tough corner of North London. But look closely at some of the 1930s mansion blocks, often regarded as among the more successful examples of inter-war social housing, and you are in for a treat. Flashes of ceramic magic adorn the façades, and sailing ships make their way across the drying yards. All the work of one of Britain's leading twentieth-century artists.

Somers Town is generally defined as the area bounded by the Euston and Pancras Roads and Eversholt Street — and has been perpetually knocked around by rail projects, latterly the development of St Pancras International.

It's one of those city centre enclaves that are not too well known. It's sizeable enough — the council ward (which takes in some adjoining areas) has more than 13,000 residents. Prestige developments such as the new Francis Crick Institute for biomedical research are starting to intrude but there's no main road cutting through the area. And while there are pockets of elegant nineteenth-century terraced housing, the bulk of the locality consists of substantial blocks of between-the-wars flats.

The first social housing in and around Somers Town dates back well over a century. But the rebirth of the area is largely credited to one man — an Anglo-Catholic clergyman, Father Basil Jellicoe. He came from an elite family (the First World War's Admiral Jellicoe was a relative), was a student at Oxford, and then decided to follow his father into holy orders and was sent as a missioner to Somers Town.

He was appalled by the poor housing and overcrowding in damp and verminous buildings. It was not simply a social outrage, he argued, but 'an outward and visible sign of an inward and spiritual disgrace.' In 1924, he helped establish the St Pancras House Improvement Society — later St Pancras Housing Association, now part of the Origin group which is still based in the area — and used his social standing to gain the attention and support of Queen Mary, the then Prince of Wales and the Archbishop of Canterbury, all of whom came to Somers Town to see what Jellicoe was up to. The Prince of Wales even turned up in the local pub — Jellicoe took over management of The Anchor in Chalton Street, simply to ensure that locals had somewhere to drink which was orderly and well-run.

Father Jellicoe — often dressed in biretta and cassock — didn't want simply to pull down the old slums, but to build a new neighbourhood for those displaced which was uplifting as well as functional. 'Housing is not enough' was his refrain, a phrase still on display in Somers Town. Jellicoe resolved — said an obituary in *The Times* — 'that he would not rest until his people had homes fit to live in, and the rehousing schemes started by his society have already provided many excellent flats, with gardens, trees, ponds, swings for the children and other amenities.' And all at a rent no more than tenants were paying for the old, insanitary housing.

The key event in Jellicoe's rebuilding of Somers Town was the ceremonial demolition by dynamite in January 1930 of a row of

dilapidated houses on Bridgewater (now Bridgeway) Street — the rite performed by the chairman of the London County Council. It was vital, Jellicoe insisted, to view this act 'in the right spirit'. It was not about blowing up an old slum, but much more 'because we want to build something really nice in its place.'

The land cleared became the site of the Sidney Street estate — the street itself disappeared altogether in the course of the development. Two months after the initial demolition, Jellicoe blessed the first bricks of flats in the 'Garden Estate', as the Sidney Street development was described.

Father Jellicoe's personal involvement with Somers Town did not last much longer. His health began to fail and he died, still in his mid-thirties, in 1935. But his dream was realised. The Sidney Street estate in particular — 250 flats in blocks, all named after saints, completed in 1938 — was a trailblazer. Play areas and communal spaces were provided, and the first wing to open, St George's, received nationwide attention as 'the first block of all electric flats in the United Kingdom'.

As part of the endeavour to provide fine design, the eminent sculptor Gilbert Bayes was commissioned to provide decorative ceramics. They are there still. Walk around this development — along Chalton, Aldenham, Bridgeway and Werrington Streets — and you can see many of them still, bursts of colour and fantasy amid solid and rather dour façades.

Bayes believed that art was for the people and not just the elite and he sought out themes which he believed would have popular appeal. Above the balconied French windows on the second floor of flats, he designed Doulton stoneware lunettes, largely based on the fairy tales of Hans Christian Andersen and the brothers Grimm. You can see scenes from Sleeping Beauty, the Princess and the Swineherd, the Little Mermaid and The Tinderbox. In this same estate, Bayes also designed a marvellous clock depicting the seasons and a statuette of St Anthony on horseback.

But this fairy tale doesn't have the happiest of endings. Among the Bayes ceramics on the estate was a beautiful virgin and child for a rooftop nursery school. While these rooms were being converted into flats recently, this exceptional piece of art, so rooted in the history of the buildings, was destroyed and disposed of — a misdemeanour which has outraged the Somers Town history society.

There was another wonderful and whimsical aspect of Gilbert Bayes's commission — he was asked to design stoneware finials for the top of the washing line posts in the drying areas of the flats. Once again he turned to fairy tales, and to saints' lives and Christmas carols, for inspiration. The poles were variously decorated with sailing ships, blackbirds, tailors, demons, roses, ducks, doves and snails. These were placed not simply on the Sidney Street estate, but on two other Somers Town estates run by the same housing association and on their estates elsewhere in North London, in Kentish Town and Tufnell Park.

Bayes also sold some of these finials at exhibitions and as garden ornaments for between six and eight guineas each. They now attract a price

of about a thousand times that amount. Over the years, all the original finials have been removed — some for safekeeping but most are missing presumed stolen. The current value of the items unaccounted for could easily top half-a-million pounds. Once again, the casual attitude of the housing association has horrified conservationists and local residents. A handful of the original ceramics are now on public display nearby at the British Library (at the back of the lower floor). The rest seem to have simply slipped from view, in some cases turning up in auction rooms.

On a more positive note, Origin has provided replicas to replace a few of the lost ceramics — and so if you venture along Aldenham Street and keep your eyes open, you will see a fleet of sailing ships on top of otherwise naked washing posts, and a central finial of a decorated Christmas tree. There's a similar, smaller, batch of finials visible from Werrington Street. On another of the association's Somers Town estates and rather more hidden away — behind the Basil Jellicoe Hall on Drummond Crescent, in the courtyard between St Joseph's and St Anne's flats — doves sit on top of posts, the tallest of which bears a carpenter's bag of tools (Joseph was of course a carpenter).

But all these posts are otherwise unadorned — no washing lines, no shirts or sheets drying in the breeze. A resident explained that no one pegs up their washing in the communal area anymore because, a bit like the Bayes finials, it gets nicked.

12 | Staged Unity

Unity Mews, in the north-east corner of Somers Town, marks the location of one of the most adventurous of London's theatres. A plaque and an inscription on the brickwork reveal that this was the location, until the mid-1970s, of Unity Theatre, perhaps the most ambitious and successful of radical theatre projects. For forty years, stars of the calibre of Paul Robeson, Alfie Bass and Bill Owen strode the stage — almost all

UNITY THEATRE, Goldington Street, N.W.1.

without pay — performing everything from Brecht to hastily-written and rehearsed political revues.

Unity Theatre started its life in 1936 in a church hall in Britannia Street off Gray's Inn Road. It was closely linked to the Communist Party and saw itself as a product of the workers' theatre movement. The following year, it moved into a disused Methodist chapel dating from the 1850s at what was then 1 Goldington Street, in use at that time as a doss house and with competing plans for it to become a warehouse or a fascist meeting hall. The place 'had potential', in estate agent parlance; in other words, it needed an awful lot doing to it before it could host its first production.

The Unity Theatre Society got in architects to advise. It would take six months work to get the building in shape, they were told, and would cost £4,000. Instead, Unity Theatre decided to use volunteer workers, advertising free beer and sandwiches for any builders, electricians, carpenters or general helpers-out who would lend a hand. 400 people stepped up, according to the *Daily Worker*. The refurbishments were completed in two months and the bill was no more than £800.

The venue could take 180 theatre-goers in the stalls and a further 150 in the balcony. The opening night, 25th November 1937, was invitation only. The London Labour Choral Union, conducted by Alan Bush, began the evening, followed by the Workers' Propaganda Dance Group performing a piece on the Spanish Civil War. Then the highlight: the incomparable American baritone Paul Robeson singing half-a-dozen spirituals — including 'Ol' Man River' with the words 'tired o' livin', scared o' dyin'' changed to 'must keep struggling until Ah'm dying' — and rounding off with a rapturously received rendition of the 'Internationale'. The evening concluded with a reprise of one of the productions which Unity had performed earlier with great success, Clifford Odets' 'Waiting for Lefty'.

After the war, the galaxy of talent associated with Unity included Peter Ustinov, Michael Gambon, Lionel Bart and Warren Mitchell. It seems to have been less successful as a nursery for women actors. For a while its leading light was Ted Willis, later a playwright and screenwriter who devised and wrote the TV series *Dixon of Dock Green*, and later still was a Labour member of the House of Lords. Under Willis's guidance, Unity briefly turned professional — but quickly reverted to relying on amateur and unpaid talent.

Unity got a lot of attention for its topical satirical revues, and in 1948 — just as the Cold War was hotting up — one of the cast of 'What's Left?', Beryl Lund, was revealed to be a civil servant working on sensitive defence contracts. Amid excited newspaper headlines, she was forced out of her job and moved to a much more mundane post at the Science Museum. She refused to say at the time whether she was a member of the Communist Party — but later cheerfully admitted that she had been.

Unity Theatre never quite regained the energy and enthusiasm it had enjoyed in the late 1930s and 1940s. But it continued to be a leading venue for radical theatre, putting on its own performances and hosting events organised by a new generation of radical theatre groups which emerged from the late 1960s. That all came to a shuddering halt when the building on Goldington Road caught fire — the cause remains a mystery — in the early hours of 8th November 1975. The roof collapsed and the auditorium was destroyed, though much of the structure survived. The building was underinsured, however, and it was clearly going to be a struggle to fund the repairs, exacerbated by political and artistic differences which had become increasingly evident among the Unity faithful.

An alliance of radical theatre groups came up with an ambitious plan to rebuild the theatre and repurpose it for an era in which old-style state socialism felt part of the problem rather than the solution. But Unity Theatre's AGM said 'no go', prompting the theatre's historian, Colin Chambers, to remark that the society's members clearly 'mistrusted outsiders even more than they mistrusted each other.'

In 1988, the plot was sold to the St Pancras Housing Association — the successor to the organisation Father Jellicoe set up in the 1920s — and the flats which now stand on the site, and host the twin memorials to Unity, were completed four years later. The Unity Theatre Trust continues to fund drama projects which have a radical or outreach aspect. Unity Theatre in Liverpool — born out of the same radical impulse that saw forty years of agitprop drama in Somers Town — is still going strong.

13 | Requiem for a Phone Box

The red phone box — remember them? — now belongs to a lost era before the digital flood. It's about as contemporary as crinoline or curled moustaches. But the genesis of this once iconic item lies in a local graveyard — and it was designed by one of an architectural dynasty who have made their mark in and around our patch.

Sir Gilbert Scott — also responsible for the Albert Memorial and the Foreign Office, and perhaps the most renowned architect of his day — designed the Midland Grand Hotel, the gloriously gothic building with clock tower which is in everyone's mind's eye when St Pancras is mentioned. The 150-bedroom hotel opened in 1873, but neither the heating nor the plumbing lived up to expectations and it closed in 1935, only coming to life again under a new name in 2011. British Rail had at one point wanted to demolish the old pile but were foiled by an energetic conservation campaign.

His grandson, Sir Giles Gilbert Scott, turned to St Pancras for inspiration for his most renowned design — the telephone box. His model was a memorial in the grounds of St Pancras Old Church. This was built by another architect, Sir John Soane, over the grave of his wife, who died in 1815. Soane himself was also buried in these vaults twenty-two years later.

The monument is, in the verdict of the architectural authority Nikolaus Pevsner, 'outstandingly interesting', which for him is praise indeed: a marble memorial with a stylishly simple canopy of Portland stone. It shares a distinction with the Midland Grand: both are Grade 1 listed.

Giles Gilbert Scott was for many years a trustee of Sir John Soane's Museum not too far away in Lincoln's Inn Fields and knew the memorial well. He had the gently curving canopy in mind when, in 1924, he submitted the winning entry of a competition to design a phone kiosk. This K2 model of the phone box, in cast iron and painted red, was installed across London.

In the mid-1930s, Scott also came up with the K6 phone box, a slightly smaller version of his original, tens of thousands of which were placed at street corners across the country. It became a familiar, defining aspect of the British streetscape, and has been widely regarded as the epitome of simple but elegant design.

The K6 was superseded only in the late 1960s. Several thousand Scott-designed red phone boxes remain in place, and even occasionally in use. In the aftermath of the Brexit referendum, the *Financial Times* described 'this most British of icons' as a perfect metaphor for the national crisis of identity. 'A shelter made for an obsolete technology in the heavy industrial heartlands of Scotland, beautifully designed but inspired by a Regency tomb from the year of Waterloo.'

14 | The Hardy Tree

The Old St Pancras graveyard closed, after many centuries of burials, in 1854. It was one of London's most overworked cemeteries — averaging in the 1830s and '40s three or four fresh interments a day. So when in the mid-1860s, a portion of the graveyard had to be cleared for the railway lines leading in to the new St Pancras Station, it was a grisly task.

The work was taken on by an architectural practice headed by Arthur Blomfield. His father had been the Bishop of London and this, it seems, bestowed on him a reputation for being decorous and respectful when doing the dirty churchyard jobs. Blomfield himself had a suspicion that, during an earlier removal of remains in another burial ground, the contractors had pulled a fast one, and disposed of bones, coffin splinters and all the unspeakable accoutrements with unseemly haste. So when he started work on clearing part of the Old St Pancras grounds, Blomfield gave one of the junior architects in his office, Thomas Hardy, responsibility for supervising the operation.

Yes, it was *that* Thomas Hardy — then in his mid-twenties, unpublished, and spending a few not always happy years in London before returning to the West Country.

For several autumn and winter months, Thomas Hardy — according to a biography by his widow which is as much an autobiography — came to Old St Pancras churchyard every evening between five and six, as well as sometimes at other hours:

> There after nightfall, within a high hoarding that could not be overlooked, and by the light of flare-lamps, the exhumation went on continuously of the coffins that had been uncovered during the day, new coffins being provided for those that came apart in lifting, and for loose skeletons; and those that held together being carried to the new ground on a board merely; Hardy supervising these mournful processions when present, with what thoughts may be imagined, and Blomfield sometimes meeting with him there.

It was a gruesome task which prompted a macabre sense of humour. 'In one coffin that fell apart was a skeleton and two skulls. [Hardy] used to tell that when, after some fifteen years of separation, he met Arthur Blomfield again and their friendship was fully renewed, among the latter's first words were: 'Do you remember how we found the man with two heads at St. Pancras?'

In his poem 'The Levelled Churchyard' — in part, surely, a reflection of his experiences at St Pancras — Hardy wrote of cadavers 'mixed to human jam'. The original version included the lines:

> Where we are huddled none can trace
> And if our names remain
> They pave some path or p---ing place
> Where we have never lain!
>
> Here's not a modest maiden elf
> But dreads the final Trumpet,
> Lest half of her should rise herself
> And half some local strumpet!

And the pissing place? Well, who knows — but there's an old ash in the burial ground surrounded by stacks of displaced gravestones. Over the decades the slabs have become entwined with the growing tree, the living and the dead locked in an evocative embrace. It's become known as the Hardy Tree, though there's no evidence that Hardy played any part in the stacking of the stones, and indeed it's possible that the sapling took root decades after the novelist's brief association with the burial ground.

This mass exhumation of bodies, in many cases not all that old and decayed, touched on popular fears of ghouls, grave robbers and noxious infection. It was the epitome of the mid-Victorian urban nightmare. The work was done at night to seek to assuage public alarm, but the use of flares and the night-time diggings and reburials simply intensified a sense

of the sepulchral. By the time St Pancras Station opened, an estimated 8,000 corpses had been disturbed. For all Blomfield's care and concern, there were complaints that the digging up and reburial had been done so unceremoniously that questions were raised in Parliament and the work halted briefly until a touch more respect was shown for the dead.

The grandest monument in the grounds, not quite so elegiac as the Hardy Tree but much more imposing, is in memory of those whose nearby graves were disturbed. The Burdett-Coutts Memorial Sundial, an obelisk erected in the 1870s at the behest of the philanthropist Angela Burdett-Coutts, lists a few dozen of the more eminent among the many thousands to have suffered that fate. The sundial bears the inscription: 'Tempus Edax Rerum' — time devours all things.

St Pancras Old Church, small and so extensively restored in the nineteenth century that it is in essence of Victorian vintage (St Pancras New Church on Euston Road is, paradoxically, older), has a real intimacy and charm. The discovery long ago of a seventh-century altar stone has encouraged speculation that there has been worship here since Anglo-Saxon, or perhaps even Roman, times.

The cemetery was declared a public park in 1877 and is now known as St Pancras Gardens. Although it's only a few minutes' walk from both King's Cross and St Pancras stations, and is among the most attractive of central London's former burial grounds, it's not that well known. The space is hemmed in by both the canal and rail lines, just to the north looms St Pancras Hospital, initially the local Workhouse, and the location here of a public mortuary and coroner's court adds to a sepulchral aura.

The recent opening of Somers Town Bridge, a foot and cycle bridge over the Regent's Canal, offers easy access from the eastern side of the cemetery to Granary Square and the newly fashionable northern environs of King's Cross. The old burial ground is no longer a dead end but a short cut.

As you might expect of a burial ground which has been bashed around such a lot, the most visited grave at Old St Pancras no longer marks the burial spot of the woman it commemorates.

Just a few feet away from the Soane family vaults lies the initial resting place of Mary Wollstonecraft, author of *A Vindication of the Rights of Woman*. First published in 1792, Wollstonecraft's celebrated book emphasises the importance of women's education. It's also much more than that, a seminal assertion of women's rights which has been an inspiration to generations of feminists and activists.

'I do not wish [women] to have power over men; but over themselves,' she asserts. 'My own sex, I hope, will excuse me, if I treat them like rational creatures, instead of flattering their *fascinating* graces, and viewing them as if they were in a state of perpetual childhood, unable to stand alone.'

The inscription on the tombstone, which specifically records her authorship of *The Rights of Woman*, was refreshed on the 200th anniversary of the book's publication — though once again it is now not easily decipherable.

Shortly after the appearance of her most celebrated work, Wollstonecraft left for Paris — just as war was looming between Britain and revolutionary France. A few weeks after she arrived, Louis XVI was guillotined. She embarked there on a turbulent romance with an American, Gilbert Imlay, with whom she had a daughter, Fanny. They never married, though Wollstonecraft sometimes styled herself 'Mrs Imlay'.

Wollstonecraft returned to London in 1795 in a forlorn attempt to revive her relationship with Imlay. She travelled in Scandinavia and published an account of her journey. On her return, she met and fell in love with the political philosopher William Godwin, author of *Political Justice* (1793) and a proponent of anti-statist arguments which contributed to the development

Mary Wollstonecraft Godwin.

London, Published 1st Copal by S.Johnson, 61 Poula, March 1798.

of anarchism. This was a much happier relationship. They were very different by character — Wollstonecraft freewheeling and Godwin rather fussy. But he loved and respected his partner and shared much of her radical and questioning attitude towards gender and the institutions that constrained women.

On 29th March 1797, the couple entered into an institution which Godwin had once described as 'the most odious of all monopolies': marriage. They did so quietly at St Pancras Old Church. 'The principal motive for complying with this ceremony,' Godwin wrote, 'was the circumstance of Mary's being in a state of pregnancy. She was unwilling, and perhaps with reason, to incur that exclusion from the society of many valuable and excellent individuals, which custom awards in cases of this sort.'

Just a few days later, Wollstonecraft and Godwin moved in to one of the earliest building projects in Somers Town, the newly-built Polygon, a ring of three-storey semi-detached houses then 'pleasantly seated near fields and nursery gardens'. Godwin also took separate rooms nearby. 'The pair shared a bed at the Polygon,' commented Janet Todd, one of Wollstonecraft's biographers, 'but when morning came, Godwin retreated to his apartment to study, write and be visited.'

The development was at first rather exclusive, but with the coming of the railways — nearby Euston station opened in 1837 — the area became crowded with those displaced, and cramped terraced housing took over much of Somers Town. The Polygon was demolished in the 1890s, but it survives in the street name Polygon Road and a block of flats there, Oakshott Court, bears a plaque to Wollstonecraft.

Their daughter, also called Mary, was born at home five months later. In Godwin's sorrowful words, as his wife entered labour 'she went up to her chamber — never more to descend.' The placenta broke apart during birth. Wollstonecraft suffered bleeding, fever and shivering fits.

She had chosen to have a woman midwife, breaking with the middle-class convention of the time. Mrs Blenkensop was the matron of a lying-in hospital and enormously experienced. It was she who, Godwin said, advised him to call in a doctor — and over the next few days he prevailed on several, some of them friends and associates, to attend on his wife. One of these doctors — in a detail which to modern sensibilities is distinctly discomforting — 'forbade the child's having the breast, and we therefore procured puppies to draw off the milk.'

Wollstonecraft didn't lack expert medical care, and while there has been a skirmish about who was to blame for her death — some historians insisting that Mrs Blenkensop was the problem and others that all would have been well if the male doctors had steered clear — there is no clear culpability. Eleven days after Mary junior was born, Mary senior died of septicaemia. She was thirty-eight. Godwin was devastated. 'This light was sent to me for a very short period, and is now extinguished for ever!'

Mary Wollstonecraft was buried on 15th September 1797 in Old St Pancras churchyard — Godwin didn't attend the funeral. Almost forty years later, he was interred in the same grave, as was his second wife, yet another Mary.

And the baby? Mary Wollstonecraft Godwin didn't get on too well with her stepmother. She would as a teenager escape from the family home in Holborn and spend time by her mother's grave, often taking a book with her. When she began a clandestine romance, the grave served as a rendezvous. Mary's lover was the poet Percy Bysshe Shelley. Her father didn't approve, above all because Shelley — an occasional visitor to the home — was married (indeed his wife was pregnant with their second child). Godwin recorded that on 26th June 1814, Shelley accompanied Mary 'to the tomb of Mary's mother... and there, it seems, the impious idea occurred to him of seducing her, playing the traitor to me, and deserting his wife.'

Godwin remonstrated with Shelley and believed that he had brought the relationship to an end. But a month later, the couple eloped to the continent. Mary was then sixteen; Shelley was twenty-one. Mary's step-sister, Claire Clairmont, also a teenager, tagged along too (and later had an affair with Lord Byron).

Mary's and Shelley's lifestyle — as you might imagine — was unconventional. They married in 1816, after the suicide of Shelley's first wife. Two years later, when Mary Shelley was twenty, she published the work for which she remains renowned, *Frankenstein* (which with its focus on death and grief bears more than an echo of her mother's demise). Four years after that Percy Shelley drowned at sea off the Italian coast. The couple had three children, of whom only one, another Percy, outlived his father.

When Mary died in 1851, it was intended that she too would be buried in Old St Pancras churchyard but her son and daughter-in-law decided that the location was too 'dreadful'. She was instead interred in a churchyard near their home in Bournemouth and the remains of her parents were dug up and reburied alongside, leaving Godwin's second wife alone and abandoned in the St Pancras grave.

But the original pedestal tomb, hewn from Portland stone, remains in place and is sometimes adorned with flowers in tribute to Mary Wollstonecraft. Not many of those who died in the eighteenth century continue to be remembered quite so warmly in the twenty-first. After a long campaign to honour her with a public sculpture, Maggi Hambling is to create a piece of art which will be a celebration of her life. The proposal is to place this not at Old St Pancras churchyard but a couple of miles away on Newington Green, overlooking the Unitarian church which she at one time attended.

16 | Cruising in St Pancras

Yes, you read that right. St Pancras really does have a cruising scene — with quite the most remarkable club room you could imagine.

When we say cruising — think canals, locks, narrowboats. What else could you be thinking of? The St Pancras Cruising Club has been going sixty years — and everyone who loves this part of London owes a debt to the club members, and to all who spend their weekends on our waterways, for their role in the resurrection of London's canal network.

In that lost era between the death of commercial canal traffic and the blossoming of leisure boating, the canals were a byword for miasma, rubbish and decay. Not any longer. The St Pancras club is one of the country's most prestigious canal boat organisations. It's based where the canal and the rail tracks run side-by-side, and that's no accident. St Pancras Basin, the club's home, dates back to the 1860s, and was where barges would load up with coal brought by train into the goods yard. By the time of the Second World War, the basin was no longer used for moving coal, and the cruising club has been based there since 1958.

'When we first joined,' a club veteran confided, 'it was a perilous journey from King's Cross station to the club, especially for a woman on her own. The canals were regarded as the back of beyond only peopled by eccentrics, layabouts and blaggards. The area was neglected. However, we could cruise and moor almost at will across London.'

The club has about a hundred members and is entirely self-supporting. Sixty or so narrow boats have moorings in the basin. There's a landscaped

canal-side garden, a lock-keeper's cottage, a dry dock... and then there's the club's superb HQ.

When the building of the Eurostar terminus at St Pancras International took all before it on the south side of the canal, some of the more iconic elements of the area's industrial landscape were found a new home. The gas works on Battlebridge Road dated back to the 1820s, and four of its huge gasholders (there were at its peak more than twenty) were transplanted to the other side of the canal. One now surrounds a small but charming park; the others provide the exterior skeletons of blocks of luxury flats.

The other item that made the leap to the Regent's canal was a stunning 1872 waterpoint, designed to supply water to the Midland Railway's steam locomotives coming in and out of St Pancras Station. Usually, these waterpoints are simply tanks. This beauty was designed by the same firm of architects that brought us the St Pancras hotel, and has brickwork — and gothic intent — to match.

It was constructed just north of the main St Pancras train shed, and so was old-and-in-the-way when the construction of St Pancras International was imminent. With the support of English Heritage, the Waterpoint was cut into three horizontal sections — the base had to be left behind and a replica was built on its new site, on top of heavily reinforced concrete slabs themselves in turn resting on a viaduct. Over three days in November 2001, the top two sections — each weighing 120 tons — were moved half-a-mile to their new home.

The uppermost of the three storeys remains a cast iron water tank complete with original ballcock and a capacity of 2,400 cubic feet. A viewing platform has been built within it offering a wonderful vantage point of the moorings on one side and the twin stations on the other. The ground floor has for some years constituted the Cruising Club's home, complete with displays recounting the twin engineering marvels of the Waterpoint and its move.

Members have been building a new club house alongside the dry dock, but will continue to have custody and the use of the Waterpoint. Sadly, apart from occasional open days, this glorious remnant of the steam age is off bounds. The Cruising Club doesn't encourage attention. The commodore and his management committee fended off our enquiries: 'Firstly the Club is not open to the public and so future readers of your book might be frustrated by being unable to visit us. Secondly we would not wish to be seen as a curiosity!'

Some club members have been a little friendlier, sharing their pride in this long-running local institution and their concern about overcrowding on the waterways — 'particularly by those who have not chosen the water but find themselves there as a last resort,' as one narrowboat enthusiast put it. And then there's the bigger issue about how the club should respond to the changes all around them. The new Somers Town pedestrian bridge across the canal has made the club and basin much more visible. That's a mixed blessing. One boat owner was awakened not long ago at three in the morning by teenagers jumping on deck in pursuit of a Pokemon.

The club is keenly aware that in other areas, when canal-side residences have gone up-market, that's often been followed by demands for the boats to move out. 'We are no longer the secret haven we were,' says one longstanding member. 'And we have to convince our new neighbours that we are not weird and threatening but cuddly and quirky'.

17 | Raving at Bagley's

The story of Coal Drops Yard mirrors all the ups and downs of King's Cross. Built in the 1850s alongside both the canal and the rail tracks to receive, sort and store the coal which powered the capital, it has over the years sunk into something close to dereliction, then bounced back as a vibrant part of the counter-culture (which is what we focus on here) and is now reborn as an upmarket retail and leisure complex. The original Victorian structures are astonishing in their scale and ambition and their refurbishment has come with a sweeping new roofscape, so that the two adjoining buildings now kiss in mid-air.

It is situated between the majestic six-floor Granary Building — one of London's most imposing industrial buildings, completed in 1852 and now the home of Central Saint Martins, part of the University of the Arts — and the equally iconic cluster of transplanted gasholders. This magnificent assembly of renovated commercial structures is the most emphatic aspect of the makeover of the railway lands north of King's Cross and St Pancras stations.

The two coal drops — vast slate-roofed three-level buildings/viaducts/ sheds constructed by the Great Northern Railway — were designed for coal wagons to enter on tracks on the top floor and drop their loads into storage hoppers which in turn fed the coal to loading carts below. The need for carriages to have access, and for air to circulate to clear the dust and fumes, meant large spaces and generous open arches. The yards could hold 15,000 tons of coal, the size of the operation reflecting the growing city's hunger for fuel. But discharging the coal in this manner tended to turn too much of it into dust. By the end of the century the greater part of the coal drops buildings had been turned into warehouses.

One of these warehouses was used by Bagley's, a Yorkshire firm which made glass bottles and decorative items and did well from the inter-war demand for inexpensive domestic glassware, specialising in art deco pressed glass. When the warehouse was taken over by a film company, the name carried on — and the early raves were advertised as at Bagley's film studios. That is the prosaic explanation of how Bagley's, the biggest London rave venue of the 1990s, got its name. In a clever echo of the King's Cross's rave era, the new raised walkway from the Somers Town footbridge over the canal and alongside the coal drops has been named Bagley Walk.

The warehouse was available at a time when legislation, and public attitudes, was pushing big raves — parties with electronic dance music and usually deep, booming bass, and quite often drugs as well — away from open air venues to indoor locations. Bagley's raves launched at the beginning of the nineties. Ryan Perry started going around 1992 when the hard core jungle scene got established and when the building still bore the trace — you might say the stain — of its original use. 'We'd walk out of there literally black. If you rubbed a wall, or if you squeezed past someone, your clothes would be black.'

Bagley's not only benefitted from a great city centre location, it also had space — lots of it. There was a capacity of 2,500, which was sometimes — perhaps recklessly — exceeded.

'First time I went in there — to a Double Dipped night — I was blown away. Thousands of people rolling round the gaffe, four rooms, a nice outdoor area where you could lie around and get fucked in those days.' Towards the end of the nineties, Perry put on his own weekly Best of British nights at Bagley's featuring jungle drum and bass. 'I've got extremely good memories of it — from partying and from putting on my own events, and going to other events. Some real big action there.'

'You'd walk in to what was generally known as the gold bar or foyer bar and there would be a DJ spinning some tunes. Upstairs you would be right in to the main room, which could take 950 people — bare brick walls, painted purple. Amazing space. Though there was no air conditioning!'

On Saturday nights, Bagley's hosted the Mud Club — which brought a touch of decadence, surrealism and design flair to the rave. And for those who revelled in the club scene, Bagley's was both a great venue and a place where new styles could emerge.

'Bagley's opened up the hardcore drum and bass crowd to the garage genres and techno due to the amount of rooms,' recalls another Bagley's regular, A.J. Dizzy Taylor, who now runs Rave Archive. 'It allowed us all to mix together under one roof. I'm still friends today with people I met there.'

'There was a small section that wasn't a music room. It had stalls and a photo booth — this was like a chill-out area in the days before the smoking ban. That was another thing that made Bagley's unique. Back then most venues were just indoors and at many other clubs if you wanted to go and get some fresh air, you were told there was no re-entry. Bagley's was the venue where people could stand outside and chat and congregate. It was the people's venue.'

Bagley's was taken over in 2003 by an entrepreneur who also owned a couple of other nearby clubs. It changed name to Canvas, and the last rave there was four years later. There's a big rave nostalgia scene online — and for ageing ravers, there's no bigger name than Bagley's.

18 | The Ice Well

It's one of London's hidden wonders: a vast well which once stored ice brought across the North Sea from Norway. The well is now incorporated into the displays at the London Canal Museum which is located on a basin of the Regent's Canal in what was once London's main ice warehouse. And there's a second well underneath the museum's floorboards.

In the nineteenth century, ice — unlikely as it may seem — was a widely traded commodity. Blocks of ice harvested from the lakes of New England were shipped to the southern US, to the Caribbean and even as far as India, where there is still an impressive 'Ice House' on the sea front at Chennai (previously known as Madras).

In the UK, the increasing demand for ice to keep food fresh, drinks cool and make ice cream was met from Scandinavia. Carlo Gatti, a Swiss-born businessman settled in London, built his canal-side ice wells from 1857. The ice came in bulk by ship from Norway where it was gathered from freshwater lakes close to the coast. The blocks were offloaded at Limehouse Basin into barges, brought along the canal to what's now known as Battlebridge Basin and stored in these cavernous wells.

The wells are ten metres in diameter, extend twelve metres below ground level and could each hold up to 750 tons of ice. Gatti used horses and carts to distribute the ice to shops and businesses across London. He also pioneered the mass production of ice cream and is credited with popularising the 'penny lick', a scoop of ice cream sold on the streets in a small glass bowl.

For centuries, the British elite had harvested ice whenever ponds and streams froze over, and most country houses had a small ice house, often cone-like in shape and extending deep into the ground to provide insulation. The ice chilled the wine and sherbets and the stopped the venison and pheasant stored in the game larder becoming too rank.

The international trade in ice made simple refrigeration available much more widely. It revolutionised the freight industry, allowing meat to be transported long distances in ice-packed train carriages and enabling the fishing fleet to store more of the catch on board and then get more of it to customers while still edible. Local butchers and

fishmongers could now keep their stock fresh for longer. It changed the way people lived their lives.

At every stage in the journey there was a lot of meltwater. But it's estimated that three-quarters of the ice harvested in Norway reached its end user. That's impressive!

Not long after Gatti constructed his ice wells, however, the first forays were made into mechanised ice production. This artificial ice was at first costly and the process unreliable. But within a decade or two the transcontinental shipment of ice became uneconomic, and eventually the regional ice trade was also supplanted.

The peak of Norwegian ice exports to Britain was reached in about 1900, but within fifteen years the trade had all but melted away, though it lingered on until 1939, when the last Norwegian ice boat was unloaded.

Gatti's wells were no longer used for storing ice after 1904. The building was extensively renovated and became a horse and cart depot, and then was used for warehousing and light engineering until taken over by the Canal Museum Trust in 1989.

Carlo Gatti is reputed to have died a millionaire. A branch of the family set up an ice cream business in South Africa which is still flourishing and boasts of having the largest ice cream factory in Africa.

19 | On the Tiles

It's not what you expect to see when you enter a local health centre, and a purpose-built one at that. But pop in to the premises on Killick Street on the south side of the Regent's Canal — you don't have to invent a malaise, just stroll in — and you will come across in the reception area a wonderful, fully restored painted tile panel dating from about 1880 and depicting this corner of King's Cross a century earlier.

The bucolic scene entitled 'Playing Bowls on Copenhagen Fields in the reign of George III' is what you might call a creative representation of the area as it once might have been. The tiles were commissioned by the distinctly non-bucolic Star and Garter. The pub has long gone but the building still stands on the junction of Caledonian Road and Northdown Street just a couple of hundred yards from where the panel is now installed.

The artist has taken the liberty, no doubt at the prompting of the patron, to include the Star and Garter in this rural idyll — though the pub itself didn't get going until some decades after the death of George III. It was up and running by 1848. The commissioning of this hugely ambitious tiled scene is a statement of the pub's social ambition and commercial success.

The panel was made by W.B. Simpson and Son, then at St Martin's Lane and still going, now based in Redhill. They used highly skilled in-house designers and craftsmen. The blank tiles were painted before firing and Simpson's used their own method of glazing which produced brilliant colours and highly glazed finishes.

Simpson's commission for public houses often dwelt on themes linked to the history of the building or the area. Many are now gone, but a handful have survived *in situ* in London pubs. They also worked on panels for theatres, courts, hospitals and a few tube stations, notably Regent's Park.

And the scene? Well, Copenhagen House was so-named, according to one account, because the Danish ambassador took refuge there during the Great Fire of London of 1666. It later became a pleasure resort and tea garden — the building in the centre of the panel is clearly a depiction of it. But it was nowhere near St Pancras Old Church, which is also shown — that's simply artistic license.

The house was demolished in the early 1850s when the 'live meat' market was moved from Smithfield to Copenhagen Fields, the area now known as Caledonian Park and set around the old market clock tower. These fields at one time extended almost as far south as Wharfdale Road. They were a famous venue for political meetings — an aspect not surprisingly absent from the tiles. In 1795, the caricaturist James Gillray enjoyed himself depicting a distinctly non-threatening rally here of the radical London Corresponding Society (on a spot completely devoid of any buildings). In 1834, a monster meeting assembled on the fields to protest against the transportation to Australia of the Tolpuddle Martyrs, agricultural workers convicted, in an attempt to break the incipient trade union movement, of swearing a secret oath..

The fields are commemorated in some local street names — and along Copenhagen Street, on the gable wall of what was once a pub, there's another splendid piece of public art. This is a huge mural by Dave Bangs commemorating the radical lineage of the area, completed in 1984 and now somewhat faded, but still very much worth seeking out

The Killick Street panel isn't at all political in its subject matter, portraying all the staples of stylish eighteenth-century leisure — men

FIELDS in the reign of GEORGE III ·

playing bowls, women sporting fans, a black page boy offering glasses of (perhaps) madeira, even a peacock. As you might expect from a commission for a public house, there's an awful lot of alcohol being consumed.

The Star and Garter housed the tiles through its heyday and into its declining years, when the pub was a focal point of the street prostitution with which King's Cross became synonymous. Last orders were called more than twenty years ago, but the rusting arm for the signboard still reveals the building's past use. Latterly it's been converted into an Islamic centre mainly serving the local Bangladeshi community and is now the al Nehar Mosque.

The panel was salvaged from the building when the pub closed. To be more accurate, it was discovered under a plywood cover by a council conservation officer. The owner had started to chip away at the tiles to try to remove them, and was happy to sell the whole lot. Even more remarkably, the local health authority agreed to find the tiles a new home and to pay for their repair.

That work was done at the Jackfield Conservation Studio in Ironbridge — and there was quite a bit of damage to make good. Lesley Durbin undertook the restoration work of what she judges to be a particularly nice piece of tile work. 'If you look along the bottom left you will see that some of the tiles are hand painted by myself, they were missing,' she says. 'It was only sheer luck that an old photograph emerged which showed that there was a little dog in the picture otherwise he would have not been included.'

It was just a coincidence — says the practice manager at Killick Street — that the health centre was being built at exactly the time the tiled panel needed a new home. The centre opened in 1997 with the restored panel on prominent display — a happy example of a piece of local art being preserved and enjoyed by the community it was designed to serve.

Just off Pentonville Road, in a former churchyard, there's a piece of public art which is more than a touch macabre. Two coffin-lid shaped metal installations lie side-by-side in the grass, and if you dance on them — or more like stamp on them — the different segments play gruff musical notes. The churchyard is now called Joseph Grimaldi Park, and one of these coffin lids is a tribute to this most famous of all clowns, who lies buried somewhere nearby. The other is to the composer and dramatist Charles Dibdin, sometimes described as Grimaldi's mentor, who — strange this! — is interred some miles away in Camden Town.

If you have the knack, you're supposed to be able to dance a musical rendition of the song Grimaldi made famous, 'Hot Codlins' (these were baked apples sold back in the day by street vendors). Though since I doubt there's anyone around who knows how 'Hot Codlins' goes, I'd say — if you are tempted to tap dance on a coffin — anything goes!

'I wanted to create something that is constantly changing,' said the artist responsible, Henry Krokatsis — 'a joyous interlude from the silence of death.' Thank you for that!

And Joey Grimaldi? In the early 1800s he developed the role of the clown as comic figure in pantomimes and on stage (not, at this time, in the circus ring) and achieved acclaim with performances at Sadler's Wells and Drury Lane. *Mother Goose* was his breakthrough show — it ran at Covent Garden for 111 performances.

Grimaldi's development of harlequinade, and his inventive use of face paint and costume, made him one of the celebrities of his era and a household name. There's a blue plaque on Grimaldi's former home in Clerkenwell's Exmouth Market. To this day, clowns are often known as Joeys.

Ill health and rickety joints forced Grimaldi to retire from the stage in 1823. He was depressive and a heavy drinker and became mired in debt. In the 1830s he moved to Southampton Street (now Calshot Street) on

the north side of Pentonville Road. Grimaldi popped in most evenings to his local, the Marquis of Cornwallis, and when he lost the use of his legs, the landlord carried him to and fro on his back.

On the evening of May 31st 1837, Grimaldi was carried home as usual. The next morning he was found dead in his room. He was buried nearby at St James's, Pentonville. As well as the installation, there's a more conventional gravestone, with railings around it decorated by the masques of comedy and tragedy — though that too doesn't precisely mark the burial spot.

St James's became known as the clowns' church, and for many years hosted an annual clowns' service. But at some time in the 1950s, the clerical incumbent cleared out the statuette of Grimaldi and photos of leading clowns complaining that they made the church porch look 'like the entrance to a picture palace'. The clowns switched allegiance to a church in Dalston. And as if cursed by their absence, St James's — a handsome chapel built in the 1780s — closed in 1978 and was demolished six years later.

Joey had the last laugh. On the exact same spot that the church once stood, Grimaldi Park House was built. The façade is a less than convincing replica of the old church, with the addition of a likeness of the great clown high above the main entrance. Otherwise it's a fairly pedestrian office building.

Most of the gravestones were cleared from the churchyard well over a century ago. It had a bad reputation. In the 1890s, it was alleged that as many as sixty or seventy sex workers used the burial ground for professional purposes, day and night. Some of this area

is now a playground, and the rest a rather nondescript park which takes the name of its most famous interment.

Every year on 31st May, the anniversary of Grimaldi's death, a handful of Joeys gather around his gravestone to celebrate the pioneer of their stagecraft. They blow a few whistles, do a couple of conjuring tricks, shuffle a few comic steps, raise a few smiles and round off the performance with the laying of a wreath. For a tribute to such an exuberant performer, it all feels a little melancholy — but then, clowns are.

21 | Mrs Wilberforce's Yard

That local cinematic classic, *The Ladykillers*, is much in evidence — in miniature — in a corner of Pentonville, just up the hill from King's Cross, where model railway enthusiasts have assembled an astonishingly detailed and ambitious layout of the tracks heading out of the goods yard. From the outside, Keen House on Calshot Street, just a rail carriage length from Pentonville Road, is about as bland and anonymous as it's possible for a building to be. Inside it's something rather unique. A place where the romance of the railways holds sway. This is the home of the world's oldest model railway club (with a *Guinness Book of Records* certificate to prove it) and the only one in purpose-built premises.

The club dates back to 1910, long before the era of Hornby and Triang and mass-produced model rail engines, at a time when this was a rich man's hobby. And the ample means of at least some of the enthusiasts allowed the club to buy its own building back in 1959.

To be more accurate, it bought a vacant plot of land which had been used during the Blitz as an emergency reservoir to fight fires. In the basement back yard, there's even now a patch of tarred wall which dates back to its wartime use. The modellers still required a loan to fund the building work — and reassured the bank that it was going to be a small factory, which was stretching it a bit.

Keen House is a sizeable place — with a layout-building room and small workshop in the basement, a couple of small rooms on the ground floor, and a hall / lecture room / common room / bar / test room on the first floor where there's also a specialist library of 4,000 volumes. The club HQ was named after a long-serving chairman, Geoffrey Keen — as in the venerated engineering, automotive and aerospace business Guest, Keen and Nettlefolds, a company which traces its roots back to the 1750s and which was renamed GKN in 1986.

The club has 250 members. Not all men, we were assured — but on the Thursday club evening when we called, there were perhaps fifty enthusiasts in attendance, with just one woman among them. Tony Cox,

89

the current chairman and an accountant, says membership is gently increasing. 'Model railways are not as popular now as in the 1960s by any stretch of the imagination,' he says, 'but we do have more members in their twenties and thirties than we used to.'

The big draw of a club with permanent premises is that there's somewhere secure to build, store and display the vast track lay-outs which are at the heart of the model railway experience. The club has some half-a-dozen of these layouts, though even here at Keen House there's only room for one to be in use at a time.

The most popular is of Copenhagen Fields, the area a little to the north of King's Cross where trains emerged from the tunnels and goods yards. Club members started planning this meticulously detailed lay-out in 1983; thirty-five years later, they say it's getting close to completion. The track, buildings, signs and people have all been hand-made — a labour of love as well as a demonstration of craft, skill and incredible stamina. The era recreated is, broadly, between the wars and the locomotives are 2mm Finescale. The layout measures about eight metres by two-and-a-half metres, and can be packed away in boxes and fitted into a Luton van to take to exhibitions. It takes five hours to put up and two hours to dismantle.

This is just the spot where the *Ladykillers* gang fall to their deaths on the tracks one-by-one, leaving dear old Mrs Wilberforce with all the loot. The modellers have worked into the layout several tongue-in-cheek references to the movie — and when they take it to events they also show *Ladykillers* out-takes of just this area.

Quite by chance, Tony Cox, the club chairman, once lived very close to Mrs Wilberforce's lopsided track-side house on Frederica Street. His old home on Bunning Way was once the site of a Great Northern Railways goods yard. The layout of course includes this much lamented feature, and indeed you can see Tony pointing to it. In a tribute to the Ealing Comedies movie, this section of the layout is known to club members as Mrs Wilberforce's Yard.

It's one of those churches that is 'more prepossessing inside than out', in the wise words of the *Survey of London*. Let's put that more emphatically. This tabernacle is distinctly drab as seen from the street, stretching awkwardly between Pentonville Road and King's Cross Road. But step in, and the building is altogether more imposing, with a spacious beam roof, splendid gallery and huge (and alas, no longer used) organ.

And hallelujah! It's still in use as a place of worship, and still meeting the purpose it's been put to for most of its existence — providing social focus and spiritual solace for incomers to London.

Battle Bridge Congregational Chapel, as this church was initially known, was built in the early 1850s but attracted only a modest number of worshippers. There was a lot of local competition. In 1889, the building was sold for £4,000 to a branch of the Welsh Congregational Union, who moved to King's Cross from an earlier chapel in Fetter Lane.

As the Welsh Tabernacle, it flourished. The church was extended in 1904, when a larger porch and lobby were built and the organ installed. That was also the year that a new pastor, Howell Elvet Lewis, took over; he presided here for the next thirty-six years. Lewis was, in the judgement of the BBC's Huw Edwards (who has a love for London's Welsh chapels) 'one of the giants of Liberal, Welsh-speaking Wales'.

The son of a Carmarthenshire farmhand, Lewis was a prolific writer of hymns and of Welsh poetry and was for several years the archdruid at the Welsh National Eisteddfod. He took the bardic name Elfed — and the church became known as Capel Elfed. Under his stewardship, says Edwards, the Welsh Tabernacle became 'one of the most dynamic and powerful churches anywhere in the country.' Services were primarily in Welsh and there's a memorial tablet in Welsh still on display.

There were at one time thirty or more Welsh chapels and meeting houses in central London serving those dislodged from their homeland by rural depopulation. These small churches were focal points for the

community — offering a network which helped newcomers to London to find homes and jobs as well as God. The purpose was social as much as spiritual and there were many couples who met at chapel.

The Tabernacle's membership peaked at over a thousand in the 1930s, as depression encouraged migration from the industrial areas of South Wales as well as from the dairy pastures and hill farms. This was the time when the London Welsh Centre was established nearby in Gray's Inn Road — it's still there, proclaiming itself to be 'the only Welsh cultural centre outside Wales', noted both for its bar and its Welsh language classes.

By the 1970s, the Tabernacle's membership was down to well under a third of its peak. The chapel no longer held the same attraction or importance for Welsh youngsters making their way in the capital. Marian

Howell started worshipping here in the late 1980s, when she moved to London to work as a nurse. She became the church secretary, but by then the decline in the size of congregation made amalgamation or closure all but inevitable.

'For me, I thought we needed to move forward. I wasn't sentimental about it because my roots weren't there. When you have sat through services in such a large building with only ten or twelve of you turning up, it was quite a depressing experience.'

In 1998, the church began hosting a South African congregation which worshipped in Afrikaans. For the first time in generations, the building was often full, and mainly of youngsters. The South African church was so successful it moved to a larger venue — and its success threw into stark contrast the slow ebbing away of the Welsh congregation.

Eventually the Tabernacle's members voted to leave the King's Cross building. The last service was held on 22nd October 2006. 'There was a good turn-out,' Marian Howell recalls. Three Welsh congregations in central London joined forces, their focus being the wonderful church at Eastcastle Street near Oxford Circus, which has been refurbished in part with the proceeds of the sale of the King's Cross site.

The church authorities — chastened by a huge row over a former Welsh chapel elsewhere in London which had been turned into a nightclub — were determined to maintain the religious purpose of the King's Cross chapel. In 2009, the evangelical Ethiopian Christian Fellowship Church bought the building and moved in. Once again, the tabernacle is flourishing.

Amharic has replaced Welsh as a language of worship, and the amplified gospel rock, the ululating congregation and the cameras providing live streaming on the web are all a striking contrast to the building's earlier incarnation. But at root, it's still fulfilling the same need — a place where newcomers can gather, practice their faith, celebrate their culture and make and meet friends.

The interior is well kept; the wooden pews, vast gallery, angel-faced corbels and other original fittings are still in place. It's an impressively smart and complete slice of Victorian non-conformity. On a good Sunday, the congregation nowadays can number 200; many more follow services online, and the back pew has a more impressive array of technical equipment than some TV studios.

And the best way to see the place? If the spirit moves you, pop along on a Sunday morning, You'll be welcomed and offered a translation of the service on headphones (in English that is, not Welsh). Marian Howell has popped in to attend service a couple of times and is comforted that her old church is still 'being used for the purpose it was built for.'

23 | Don't Think Twice

Shortly before Christmas 1962, a twenty-one-year old American pitched up at a folk club held at the Pindar of Wakefield, a pub towards the northern end of Gray's Inn Road. The bouncer on the door was minded not to let him in, but Peggy Seeger — who ran the club along with another soon-to-be folk legend, Ewan MacColl — insisted that he should be admitted.

The visitor played a couple of songs in the 'open mic' second-half of the evening, extending well over the normal five minutes allocated for such contributions. And the songs he played? Well, no one is absolutely sure — but one of those present has a distant recollection of hearing 'Masters of War' and a protracted version of 'The Ballad of Hollis Brown'.

This was Bob Dylan on his first visit to Britain. The pub, now called the Water Rats (it was bought in 1986 by an entertainment industry fraternity-cum-charity called the Grand Order of Water Rats) is still a music venue. And it loudly proclaims that it hosted Dylan's first British gig. Mind you, it also says that both Karl Marx and Lenin drank here — claims which, a bit like the Dylan one, may be true but are not watertight. 'Definitely Maybe', in the words of the Oasis album title — a band that really did play its first London gig here.

By the time Bob Dylan arrived in London, he had released his first album, which only sold a few thousand copies, and had recorded much of his second, including the classics 'Blowin' in the Wind', 'A Hard Rain's a Gonna Fall', and 'Don't Think Twice, It's Alright'. 'The Freewheelin' Bob Dylan' was eventually released the following May. His performances in the folk clubs and coffee bars of New York's Greenwich Village had burnished his reputation. He was getting noticed — and had, in Albert Grossman, a new manager with a knack for making stars.

That probably explains why the BBC paid for Dylan to come over at the close of 1962 to take part in a TV play, *Madhouse on Castle Street*. He couldn't act, which seems to have come as something of a shock to the play's director, but four of his songs featured in the drama. No copy of the programme survives — with culpable stupidity, the BBC wiped the tape in 1968 even though Dylan had by then become a superstar.

While in London, Dylan played no formal concerts, but he did get involved in the very active folk and blues scene and, guitar in hand, turned up at several club evenings. It's difficult to be sure where he first performed in public. Some suggest that it was the King and Queen in Fitzrovia; one Dylanologist believes it may have been the Troubadour coffee house in Earl's Court. But his contribution at the Pindar of Wakefield, on 22nd December at the Christmas get together of the

Singers' Club, is the one most talked about — not least because a photographer, Brian Shuel, happened to be in attendance.

The Singers' Club had a reputation for a rigid insistence on authenticity in folk music, while Dylan was moving away from singing the folk canon to writing his own compositions in a style influenced by traditional folk. Ewan MacColl was later rudely dismissive of Dylan, and the photos taken that evening are — some folk music experts insist with a smile — the only ones with the two singers in the same frame. (MacColl is on the far right of the photo with a beard and his eyes shut — the bald man above Dylan's head is the renowned A.L. 'Bert' Lloyd). Dylan too wasn't always smitten with the music he heard played, and at another London venue, perhaps after imbibing too much, he loudly dismissed the singer on stage as 'fucking shit'.

But where was that first public performance? Brian Shuel says that four days before the Singers' Club Christmas 'do', he was at the King and Queen to photograph Martin Carthy when Dylan turned up unexpectedly and sang a couple of songs. So that sorts it! Not quite — because as Shuel himself says, there's a suggestion that Dylan came to an earlier session of the Singers' Club at the Pindar of Wakefield and, after an informal audition, was allowed to perform a single number. It's one of those mysteries which is unlikely ever to be settled.

While on this side of the Atlantic, Bob Dylan met such luminous talents as Martin Carthy and Bob Davenport and critics agree that his exposure to English folk music helped to shape the sound and style of Dylan's music. Such classics as 'Girl from the North Country' and 'Boots of Spanish Leather' are seen as bearing the mark of his few weeks in the UK.

The Water Rats is on firmer ground in insisting that it hosted the Pogues' first ever gig in October 1982. The band is quintessentially Irish, but the King's Cross area was their home patch. Shane MacGowan was living at the time in a short-term let above a corner shop in Cromer Street, and had already been banned from most of the local pubs; two

others of the original line-up were dossing nearby in Whidborne House.

With their debut gig looming, the band plumped on the name Pogue Mahone, a phrase lifted from James Joyce's *Ulysses* which means kiss my arse in Irish Gaelic. They later became simply the Pogues because some at the BBC were reluctant to play their music after complaints (mainly from speakers of Scots Gaelic) about the vulgar name.

The Pogues secured a weekly slot at the pub — 'raucous events' according to one of the band. And it's where they met to discuss plans and to drink. The accordionist, James Fearnley, at first saw the band as 'not much more than a product of our locality, of the sisterhood of grim tenement buildings on Cromer Street, and the Norfolk Arms, the Boot and the Pindar of Wakefield.'

Their first single, 'Dark Streets of London', was all about drinking, gambling, singing and then, when winter sets in, finding —

I'm buggered to damnation
And I haven't got a penny
To wander the dark streets of London

It sounds like an elegy to their time in King's Cross!

24 | Tea Dances at the Bell

'The Bell was the opposite of cool,' insists Jarlath O'Connell, who for several years spent every Sunday there. 'Pretty young gay people getting ahead wouldn't be seen dead there. It was a real dump. The decor was shocking. It was painted black — the windows were blacked out — it stank — the toilets were disgusting. But because it was so crowded, you didn't really notice.'

It was built 160 or so years ago as a gin palace on Pentonville Road (it's now a bar called Big Chill), and said to have been designed by Stephen Geary who was also responsible for the ill-fated statue of George IV. It had become, like the area, distinctly seedy but had two huge plus points: it was easy to get to and there was a big dance floor.

From the early 1980s — when the gay community was reeling from the shock of HIV/AIDS and the stern disapproval of a Conservative government which went on to pass the notorious 'Section 28' — the Bell became a sanctuary. It was at the heart of the gay scene — a place where dancing and politics came together.

The pub was home to an array of gay sub-cultures, and there were different styles of music every night. 'The weird thing about the Bell,' says O'Connell, nowadays a part-time theatre critic, 'is you would talk to people who went there — they'd talk passionately about the place on their evening but would know nothing about what happened on other nights.'

There were the regular whip-rounds to support Gay Switchboard, the Terrence Higgins Trust (an HIV and sexual health charity which started in 1983) and — during the 1984 85 strike — Lesbians and Gays Support the Miners. Among many of the men who came along, there was an informal style: 501 jeans, Oxblood Doc Marten boots, checked shirt, denim or bomber jacket, a few badges. And the big cultural divide was how you did your hair — floppy or waxed flat top. Goths came along too, with a very different dress sense — the various tribes eyed each other warily.

The Bell also had regular women-only nights — with women DJs playing music by bands such as Siouxsie and the Banshees. 'There was a disabled toilet in the ladies' loos,' one regular attender recalls, 'and you would see women going in there for sex. Then twenty minutes later a very upset woman would come in from the bar looking for her girlfriend.'

Jarlath O'Connell didn't get to know the Bell until the early nineties — when he became part of one of the pub's most successful institutions. In those days, Sunday licensing hours were very restricted. When the bar closed at 2pm, the dancing lessons started. Jo Purvis was in charge — 'a butch dyke and a gay legend,' as O'Connell remembers her. Jo would come along 'looking like the mafia', dressed in a suit and carrying two big record cases. The dancing style was mainly ballroom and Latin, and the music varied from classic 1950s to Motown.

The place was packed — men and women in roughly equal

LESBIANS BENEFIT FOR THE MINERS

Wednesday 6 March
8pm
Women's night
at The Bell
Pentonville Road
(Kings Cross tube)
£1.50 UB40
& £2.50 waged

Gymslips Dianne
Tapanda Re Strange
Language
Sleeze
Sisters
and
others

organised by LESBIANS AGAINST PIT CLOSURES & LESBIANS AND GAYS SUPPORT THE MINERS

full access for disabled

numbers, all ages, and quite a few transvestites, who were straight (and changed in the ladies loos, which didn't always go down well). You weren't expected to come accompanied, and were required to keep changing your same sex dance partner through the three-hour session.

At 5pm, the tea dance got going — complete with stewed tea and cucumber sandwiches. 'There was something wonderfully perverted about taking something so bourgeois and recreating it in dingy King's Cross with a load of queers.' When the bar opened at 7pm, the music got a touch more modern and raucous, and many of the tea dancers stayed on.

'Our night was a motley collection of weirdos, people who didn't quite fit in to the gay scene,' says O'Connell. And they were fiercely loyal to the Bell. 'I was religious about it. I went there at two o'clock on a Sunday and I didn't leave before midnight — that was every Sunday for quite a long time. If you went away for a week, you'd want to be back for Sunday.'

The Bell was one of the places where the same sex competitive dance scene was born — but those Sunday sessions were social dances not competitions. 'It was the only place in London where people were friendly and not on the pull,' O'Connell recalls. 'And it's one of the few places where gay men and lesbians got to meet.'

The Bell closed in 1995 and the Sunday tea dance had to find a new home — eventually settling down at a gay pub in Limehouse. O'Connell still dances. And he still misses the Bell. 'It changed my life in terms of the people I met.'

25 | Crescent Magic

If you are looking for a touch of magic around King's Cross, head to Keystone Crescent. It's an elegant, complete, hidden away semicircle of early Victorian workers' housing. Twenty-four houses, inner and outer circles, with a formidable curve: 'the smallest radius of any crescent in Europe' says a board which summarises the street's history... we'll take that on trust.

Bob Stuckey, a musician who lives in the outer circle, says the tight curve makes the street more friendly. 'It creates a village feeling. There's something about the dimensions that makes you want to say hello.' He's lived in the Crescent — a 'fantastic' spot — for more than fifty years. And he has a special connection to the place: his great-great-grandfather built it.

In the mid-1840s, Robert James Stuckey, the son of a Shoreditch bricklayer, built what was then Caledonia (later Caledonian) Crescent — the old name is still visible on a sign at the north end of the street. It took its name, as did Caledonian Road and Caledonia Street, from the nearby Caledonian Asylum for Scottish children.

The indefatigable Stuckey also built almost a hundred other properties in the area. It was a bold speculative move, probably influenced by the impending development of King's Cross Station — the Great Northern Railway was established by Act of Parliament in 1846 and its London terminal opened six years later. And it paid off — big time.

Stuckey's burst of construction work shaped the southern end of Caledonian Road. Unlike many builders, who sold their properties as soon as they could, Stuckey rented out his houses. 2A Caledonian Crescent became his estate office. The family still owns seven buildings in the Crescent — two of which are home to the builder's direct descendants — as well as a swathe of commercial properties nearby on Caledonian Road and a warehouse (part of a former bus garage) on Omega Place.

The houses on the outer circle have four floors, including a basement, with originally two rooms on each and a common toilet and wash-house in the back yard; the inner circle has three floors, and — because of the tight radius — slightly more cramped rooms and a smaller back garden.

Bob's father was born in 2A and, at his request, his body lay in rest there so that friends and tenants could pay their respects. Later, when clearing up the place, Bob found a remarkable cache of letters under the bed dating back more than a century — these were written by Robert James Stuckey, the man who built the Crescent, to his young grandchildren. That prompted Bob, himself the grandchild of one of these grandchildren, to pursue the story of the Crescent and its begetter.

These houses were not built for single families. Right from the start, they were in multiple occupation. Bob Stuckey has been through the 1851 census returns for the street. Five years after the houses were built, all but two were occupied; some had as many as seventeen people living in them. In total, 240 people, constituting seventy-six families, lived in the twenty-two properties. The occupations given suggest that these were the homes of artisans and their families, with carpenters and masons particularly well represented.

No one knows why Robert James Stuckey took to building a crescent rather than on a more conventional grid. It was perhaps the best (in other words, most profitable) use of an irregularly sized patch of land. The houses don't seem to have much in the way of foundations, but they have stood the test of time.

That's no thanks to Algernon Stuckey, the builder's grandson, who was minded to pull down the Crescent. By the Edwardian era, the houses were a little down-at-heel. A report in the *Builder* in 1891 described an overcrowded street with inadequate drainage, abutting on open land used to keep poultry and ducks, pigeon coops and rabbit hutches, which the journal pointed out was 'without advantage... to the night's rest of the neighbours'.

Algernon was as much concerned by the poor reputation of the area as a result of street prostitution. He was foiled in his redevelopment plans but did manage to rebrand the street. In 1917 it was renamed Keystone Crescent, the name reflecting a family interest in freemasonry in which the keystone is an important symbol.

Slightly tucked away but close to pubs and stations, it's easy to see why the Crescent attracted sex workers. And the renaming hardly kept the sex trade at bay. When Bob Stuckey moved in, back in the 1960s, prostitutes would routinely bring their clients to the basement yards. 'Sometimes they didn't even bother to go down to the basements.'

Keystone Crescent had also to weather a long period of planning blight. King's Cross was at one time lined up as the terminus for the Channel rail link, and that would have involved the demolition of the entire street. But it's now safe and indeed listed. The sex workers have moved on. The worst the residents face now are youngsters gathering a little out of general view to smoke dope or to drink and carouse into the small hours. That hasn't stopped prices for those Keystone Crescent properties that come on the market reaching seven figures. I imagine that Robert James Stuckey — now in a vault in the old wing of Highgate cemetery — will be pleased that his crescent has come into style.

26 | Seedy — with Character

When in 2015 the pub at the bottom end of Caledonian Road reverted to its original name, the Scottish Stores, it excited a lot of attention. Not so much because an old inn was being lovingly restored, with a listed interior and a CAMRA-approved makeover. More that the Flying Scotsman, the name by which the pub had been known since some time in the 1980s, had been banished and with it the sleazier, more disreputable aspect of the King's Cross area.

The Flying Scotsman was a strip pub — and about as basic as you can get, with its blacked-out windows, decaying decor and signs warning 'STRICTLY <u>NO CONTACT</u> WITH THE DANCERS'. The place 'smells of stale alcohol and farts,' wrote one less-than-impressed visitor, 'offering red-faced, tooled-up football away fans flat lager and semi-naked women'.

The Scotsman has gone, but its Twitter feed @Scotsmankingsx survives as a digital apparition of the pub's previous avatar. Until its abrupt end in October 2015, the tweets consist simply of running orders of that day's strippers: '1 Vicky 2 Carolina 3 Jessica Estrella Hayley 4 Ola Sophie 5 Rose Gabi Andrea'.

'It was always a little dirty,' says Tequila Rose, who spent six months working at the Scotsman just before it closed. 'I think seedy with character is the best way to describe it — and I mean that as a good thing. When you went on stage you just plugged your phone into the sound system. The customers were a real mix of dedicated regulars and locals, people travelling via King's Cross, a lot of rowdy football supporters — but all-in-all a pretty good crowd.'

There was no security, no bouncer and no DJ. 'There were definitely disputes and guys getting out of line,' Tequila Rose recalls, 'but usually the girls would back each other up and the bar staff would jump in if

necessary.' Apart from a small house fee, the strippers got to keep what they collected. They went round the pub after their act with a plastic glass and there was an understanding that everyone had to put in at least a pound coin. 'There was one area where you really couldn't see the stage and if the customer was standing there they didn't need to pay, though many of them did.'

The pub was involved with the sex trade long before it was renamed the Flying Scotsman. Daisy Louisa Hunt remembers her aunt and uncle running what was still then the Scottish Stores and living on the premises during the Second World War. 'Aunt Bet always said the pub was a finishing school. Prostitutes; gangs; soldiers; gays,' she recalls (her account has been posted at *itsjustthewaythingswere.com*). 'There were a few locals but it

wasn't the sort of pub where a local could sit and drink properly. Most people were passing through. It wasn't a comfortable place really, with the fights and the prostitutes. The prostitutes were lovely girls, they really was. It was a well-known prostitute area. The soldiers would come off the trains.'

The pub was built with style and the renovation is certainly a revelation. It dates back to 1901 and there is a real charm in the wooden panels, bar divides and all the other details brought back to life. But the demise of the Flying Scotsman caught attention because, in the words of the local paper, 'it marked the end of a long-standing connection between the sex industry and the Caledonian Road.' The sex shops, strip joints, adult cinemas — all gone! It's not that sex establishments have entirely disappeared from the area — there are still a few on Eversholt Street, opposite Euston Station. But this was a landmark in the cleaning up of King's Cross.

Not everyone is toasting that achievement. 'I prefer it as it was. That place provided a steady income to quite a few girls,' Tequila Rose insists.

'There were only stage shows at the Scotsman — no VIP or lap dancing. It was a much nicer working environment than the big clubs that take a commission on your earnings and fine you for not painting your nails or for looking at your phone.'

'I think it's a shame that getting rid of sex shops and strip clubs is seen as cleaning up. And actually all it does is drive it underground where there are fewer barriers and less transparency and regulation.'

Those local to the area have a different take. Paula McGinley lived on the southern end of Caledonian Road at a time when 'the Cross' was at its most dissolute. She recalls the Flying Scotsman as a 'notorious' strip joint which added to the area's red light reputation. The big problem, though, was the street prostitution and the kerb crawlers they attracted and the detritus of used condoms and needles left behind.

'Prostitution was evident wherever you turned. You'd go into a corner shop for a pint of milk and it was pretty obvious that the woman buying sweets was a prostitute and the guy with her was her pimp. Walking down the street at night, cars would constantly slow down and fling open the door of the passenger seat.'

But through it all she says, a sense of community survived. And in spite of being offered just about every drug imaginable and routinely being asked 'how much?', Paula found it a safer place at night than the empty suburban streets. 'I never really felt threatened. There was usually a visible police presence — and the pushers and girls weren't interested in the likes of me!'

27 | The Pacifist and the Exorcist

Housmans and the peace movement have been, from the start, part of the same fabric. 5 Caledonian Road, the site of Housmans bookshop for almost sixty years, is known today as Peace House. Spread over six floors, it has provided a home and a refuge for a huge range of anti-war and allied causes. Nowhere has been more important in sustaining a radical tradition in London.

But exorcism? It's not that there's a necessary contradiction between pacifism and exorcism — just that they don't have any obvious common ground. Yet Peace House would never have been established without the support of an exorcist.

In the months after the Second World War, Housmans Bookshop — linked to Dick Sheppard's Peace Pledge Union — was set up in war-damaged premises on Shaftesbury Avenue. It took its name from Laurence Housman, a writer and longstanding socialist and sponsor of the PPU (and younger brother of A.E. Housman, author of *A Shropshire Lad*). So it should really be Housman's — but it isn't. No one knows why there's no apostrophe.

After three years, the shop closed because of spiralling rents. But the business kept going, largely as a mail order service and by providing bookstalls for meetings and events. It shared first-floor rooms on Blackstock Road in Finsbury Park with *Peace News*, which started in the mid-1930s.

Towards the end of the 1950s, the intensity of the Cold War and the alarming prospect of nuclear conflict led to a resurgence of the peace movement and loud demands for nuclear disarmament. Leafing through back issues of *Peace News* — and what a good paper it was, published weekly (it now comes out every two months) and costing sixpence — you get a sense of the temper of those times.

The first Aldermaston march was staged in Easter 1958. The initial event was a march to the Atomic Weapons Research Establishment in this small Berkshire village (subsequent marches were from Aldermaston to London). It was staged by the Direct Action Committee against Nuclear War. At an organising meeting in Blackstock Road early that year the artist and activist Gerald Holtom came with his initial design for what is now universally known as the peace symbol — based on the semaphore signals for 'N' and 'D'. The newly-formed Campaign for

Sahara A-bomb pro

17 GOING W

ALL SET FO

FINAL PREPARATIONS WERE BEING
PROTESTS TEAM'S START TO-MO
FRENCH ATOM BOMB TESTING GR

1223 Dec. 4, 1959 6d. US Air Express
Edition 10 cents

Dora Dawtry, bookshop manager, turns the key at the opening of Housmans Bookshop, which forms part of the new Peace News premises at King's Cross, London. With her left to right are: Arthur Goss, the Rev. Tom Willis (whose gift of £5,700 made the purchase of the building possible), Frank Dawtry, Harry Mister, Vera Brittain, Hugh Brock, Sybil Morrison and Stuart Morris.

Nuclear Disarmament held its first public meeting in February 1958 and took over organising the Aldermaston marches from 1959 onwards. Roger Mayne's powerful photographs of that second march took up much of *Peace News*'s front page.

Two weeks later, the paper announced the prospect of 'a new home for *Peace News*'. Tom Willis, a curate in East Yorkshire, had just received an inheritance of £10,000 and wanted to give a donation which would make a difference to the anti-war campaign. He quietly asked a couple of peace organisations what use they would make of a sizeable gift. Harry Mister, the manager of Housmans, came up with a concrete proposal: to buy the freehold of a central London property which would act as offices, bookshop and resource centre for the peace movement.

Tom Willis eventually provided £5,000 (the equivalent today of £120,000) to buy 5 Caledonian Road. A group of young volunteers lived in the building while they were doing it up. It had previously been a kitchen shipping out ready-cooked meals. In July 1959, *Peace News* moved in — and within days reported its first overseas visitor at the new address, an Indian activist, Vimala Thakar. By November, the work was complete and Housmans opened for business. *Peace News* published a photo of the opening ceremony attended by Tom Willis sporting his dog collar and by the renowned writer and pacifist Vera Brittain. Willis had intended to remain anonymous but said he was outed to the press by Vera Brittain, which led to a touch of embarrassment — his family weren't too pleased and his parishioners wanted to know why he wasn't giving the money to church funds.

Pentonville Road was at that time — Harry Mister told the King's Cross Voices oral history project — a successful retailing area with a Lyons tea house, a branch of Hepworths the outfitters, and big name jewellers. 5 Caledonian Road was an easy spot for people to get to and the Peace Pledge Union, the Movement for Colonial Freedom and the Independent Labour Party, all, then, significant operations, had offices close by.

'First of all, Housmans was only the front bit of the ground floor — we took on a stationery side and general books for the local community as well as our pacifist stock,' Mister recalled. *Peace News* had most of the rest of the building. London CND made good use of one of the basement rooms; a pacifist publisher had a toe-hold on an upper floor; and there were tenants, 'a charming old couple', at the top.

From selling stationery and office supplies to King's Cross businesses, Housmans veered a generation later into what you might call anarcho-punk. Malcolm Hopkins, a now retired Housmans veteran, has fond memories of touring the country with the band Crass, setting up book and literature stalls at squats and other unlikely spots where the group found an audience.

Housmans now vies with the anarchist Freedom Bookshop for the title of the country's oldest radical bookshop and with Liverpool's News from Nowhere for that of the biggest. Although the peace movement owns the property, so Housmans has the cushion of an understanding landlord, it's faced some bumpy times.

'There was a moment thirteen or fourteen years ago when we were in a lot of trouble,' says Nik Gorecki, the longest-standing member of staff. 'We were on the verge of closing. We decided to concentrate on what we do best — so we made a conscious decision to only stock books that fit our political profile.'

Since then, the bookshop's books have — usually (but not always) — balanced. It has four staff, their pay pegged to the London Living Wage, and also relies on volunteers who work for not more than half-a-day a week. Almost every evening there are meetings, book groups, events and book launches in the shop.

The rooms above and below have over the decades been a base for dozens of campaigning organisations that would otherwise have struggled to find offices, including the Gay Liberation Front, the London Lesbian and Gay Switchboard, War Resisters' International, Campaign Against the Arms Trade, Pax Christi and the King's Cross Railways Lands Group. When in 1975 the British Withdrawal from Northern Ireland Campaign issued a leaflet headed 'Some Information for Discontented Soldiers' — for which fourteen defendants were tried for incitement to disaffection, and acquitted — 5 Caledonian Road was the address from which the successful defence campaign was run. *Peace News* moved to Nottingham in the 1970s but is now based once more on the Caledonian Road.

London Greenpeace (unrelated to the global Greenpeace) was based in the building as was the linked McLibel campaign — attracting so many alleged spies from the police, security services and McDonalds that at some meetings, it's been suggested, there may have been more agents than activists. Housmans now sports a blue plaque with a difference, endorsing the Campaign Opposing Police Surveillance (COPS) — address, inevitably, 5 Caledonian Road — and recording that 'Peace, Environmental and Animal Rights Campaigns meeting here were spied on by undercover police officers...'

When Housmans held a party to celebrate their 50th birthday at 5 Caledonian Road, Tom Willis came along, happy that his gift had delivered such a dividend. 'It's been a marvellous thing to see the list of some fifty organisations who have used *Peace News* offices and rooms,' he told Emily Johns of *Peace News*. 'And so I'm really pleased to see how much it has been used and how many organisations it helped.'

Willis — who died in 2014 — achieved renown in a very different area of endeavour. Yes, he was the exorcist — indeed the *Daily Mirror* described him as 'Britain's leading exorcist'— with half-a-century of experience in driving out ghosts and poltergeists. He was for many years the Archbishop of York's official adviser on occult disturbances. 'Ghosts certainly do exist,' he insisted. 'If you suspect there's evil around, don't attempt to deal with it [yourself].... When a clergyman comes to perform an exorcism, you'll need to celebrate communion in your house, commanding any evil to depart and any restless soul to go in peace to that place appointed for it.'

So he was both peacenik and ghostbuster — but Emily Johns recalls that when they met, the clergyman seemed 'more excited about exorcism than about the peace movement.' Pacifying poltergeists is, after all, probably a lot easier than achieving global peace.

28 | The Lighthouse

Of all the buildings that have gained a new lease of life in and around King's Cross, the Lighthouse has seen the most Lazarus-like resurrection. Prior to its rebuild, the fabric was, say the architects, 'in extremely poor condition and rapidly deteriorating.' A conservation officer confided that he had never seen a commercial building in central London in such a state of dereliction. Listed in 1997, it promptly went on to the 'at risk' register. And it was difficult to reprieve — for the whole edifice, four storeys and six bays, rested on not one but two shallow London Underground tunnels

The Lighthouse, a wedge-shaped building, lies at the heart of King's Cross, on the crossroads where the king's statue once stood. It creates a trinity with those two more imposing pinnacles — the high-wire gothic St Pancras hotel and the elegantly understated King's Cross Station. Its slender tower, about eight metres proud, is a local icon. But it's amazing how little we know about the back story of this landmark.

When was it built? Ah... Who by? Well... And what's the Lighthouse tower all about? Hmm...

So let's try to fill out the account. The site was cleared in 1860 or thereabouts for the building of the Metropolitan Railway, the world's first underground line. Though as anyone who has made the journey between King's Cross and Farringdon will know, it's not very far under ground. This was cut-and-cover tunnel construction. The Metropolitan had its own King's Cross Station (long demolished, it stood close to King's Cross Bridge, the southern spur to Caledonian Road) and to its west, bounded by Gray's Inn and Pentonville Roads, was a tapered plot which became known, for obvious reasons, as 'the tongue'.

Neither archives nor the local press provide any information about the construction of the building which took up the larger part of this site. The most exhaustive account of its history — an article by David Hayes in the *Camden History Review* — concludes that work was completed by 1875, and that the tower was very probably there from the start. The tower's wooden frame was originally clad in slate, though within a decade

or so that had been replaced by a zinc casing. It's octagonal with tiny porthole-style windows which add to the nautical flavour. While anyone glancing up will think 'Lighthouse', the tower's design doesn't seem to be based on any functioning lighthouse — not least because their purpose requires lots of glass to ensure visibility, not simply peepholes.

Of the many theories to explain why someone went to the enormous effort of putting up a two-storey rooftop tower to no obvious purpose, the most popular is that it brought a flavour of the coast to King's Cross and so promoted a street level oyster bar (at a time when oysters were much more widely consumed and competitively priced than now). Some versions suggest that a beacon shone from the tower whenever a fresh batch of seafood came in. The trouble is the oyster bar didn't open until the 1890s. And the tower windows are so small that any light would hardly be sufficient to beckon the hungry.

Let's take evidence from one of the few people who has been in, and on, the tower. Anurag Verma was the lead for Latitude architects on the reconstruction of the Lighthouse. He says there was a trapdoor giving access to the base of the tower, but no ladder or other means of getting up to porthole level and no sign of any light or electrical installation. 'You couldn't get into the top part physically unless you sent a child up there — from the inside, the tower is just too narrow,' Verma says. 'My take on it is that it's simply a folly'.

That seems the most likely explanation. A folly, that is, in the architectural sense of being decorative rather than functional — but whoever came up with the idea to grace the top of a curved, tight-cornered building in this manner brought a touch of stardust to what might have been humdrum, which isn't a folly at all.

There's a bigger story about the regeneration of the Lighthouse. In its long decades of decline and neglect, the building housed cheap eating places and the sort of shops and offices which wanted somewhere central and ultra-cheap. Readers of a certain vintage may recall the near-legendary Mole Jazz store on the Gray's Inn Road side of the building;

115

those of an activist persuasion may have called on the pro-choice National Abortion Campaign offices on the floor above.

Nick Capstick-Dale of UK Real Estate started buying some of the smaller buildings in King's Cross just as the wider regeneration of the area edged into view. 'My timing was quite lucky,' he concedes. His early investment in the area helps to explain his appearances in 'rich lists'. He's an enthusiast for the new King's Cross and for an overall design vision which he sees as restoring the social to a neighbourhood that seemed to be struggling.

Capstick-Dale bought the Lighthouse from P&O — another nautical link there — in 2006. He has a track record of turning round down-at-heel listed buildings by preserving their external architectural integrity but pulling out their innards. After a lot of wrangling with Camden Council, that's what he was given the green light to do here. Building work started only in 2014 and took more than two years.

The practical difficulty was the rail lines below. Steel girders in the basement rested directly on the crown of one tunnel and just a few feet above another. 'It's quite an experience being in the basement as a train goes past,' says Andrew Gilbert, founder and director of Latitude. 'With all the noise and vibration, it feels just like being on the station platform.'

The finished building needed to weigh no more, and no less, than the original. And to ensure that there was no disturbance of the tunnels, the weight on them needed to be more-or-less constant throughout the construction process — which meant working bay-by-bay rather than floor-by-floor. The girders were eventually encased in concrete. The original façade of the building was maintained as of course was the tower, but an entirely new edifice took shape within that shell.

To absorb the shake, rattle and roll, huge rubber pads were installed in the basement and anywhere the new construction touched the old. 'All the original fabric vibrates,' Gilbert says. 'All the new fabric doesn't.'

The tower, of course, was part of the original build. Much of its timber frame, though weathered, was sound. The fish-scale zinc plating was renewed, and the original cornice, railing and weather vane restored. Although the trap door into the tower was closed up, the room that allowed that access was maintained, complete with original fireplace. It's now a meeting space.

Not everyone likes the eye-catching vaulted and stepped roof, set back from the tower but in a matching zinc finish and inevitably competing with it for attention. The saving grace — for those who work there at least — is a terrace surrounding the tower with access from the new roof space. A series of glass acoustic doors dampens the vibrations from the tower to adjoining areas. And the design adds to the floor space.

The Lighthouse now provides well over 2,000 square metres of retail and office space, most of it taken as the European HQ of the music video streaming service Vevo, a tenant which fits well with the digital giants now making their homes in King's Cross. The architects reckon that keeping the original façade and the other constraints of the site and its listed status added at least a third to the overall building costs. Worth every penny!

ACKNOWLEDGEMENTS

Brian Kelly, a distinguished TV cameraman and talented photographer, has taken several of the more memorable photos in this book, once again making the 'curious' remarkable. I'm very grateful. Martin Plaut, co-author of *Curious Kentish Town* and *Curious Camden Town*, was a huge support in the compiling of this latest Curious venture. Alan Dein, who is working on *Curious Golders Green*, has been generous with his knowledge of the area. The King's Cross Voices project of which Alan was a key part is an invaluable resource for those interested in the history of the area. My thanks too to Polly Rodgers and King's Cross Story Palace, a Heritage Lottery funded project in partnership with Historypin and the Building Exploratory.

Elly Clarke's photograph of Nasim Ali in the council chamber of Camden Town Hall is included with her kind permission. The stills from and publicity shots for *The Ladykillers* are courtesy of StudioCanal Films Ltd. The photograph of Tony and Caroline Benn and the occupiers of Holy Cross Church was taken by the King's Cross AV Collective — I'm grateful to the English Collective of Prostitutes for permission to include it. The Unity Theatre Trust kindly agreed to the inclusion of photos of and relating to Unity Theatre. The photo of Bagley's in 1994 is courtesy of DJ Andy Ward. Peter Willis took the photo of the tiles now housed in the Killick Street health centre and gave permission for it to be included in this book. The photograph of Bob Dylan performing at The Pindar of Wakefield is reproduced with the kind permission of Brian Shuel and Collections. The images of the Flying Scotsman are courtesy of @erntsgraf. The reproduction of part of the front page of *Peace News* is with the publication's consent: www.peacenews.info. Photographs of the tower of the Lighthouse Building are with the kind permission of Gilbert McCarragher and Latitude architects. My thanks to Paul Day for permission to use a close-up of his lovers' sculpture at St Pancras Station. The aerial photo on the rear cover is courtesy of A.P.S. (UK).

Nancy Edwards has designed the map for this book, as she has for all the 'Curious' titles so far. My warm thanks also to Pippa Hennessy for the design of this book and for Ross Bradshaw of Five Leaves Publications for keeping faith with the 'Curious' venture

Across 'the Cross' and beyond, I've benefitted from the kindness, hospitality, recollections and advice of many who have a stake in the area and its buildings and institutions — this is a much better book for their help. Thank you! A particular word of gratitude to Malcolm Holmes, a former Camden borough archivist, and to Tudor Allen and all the staff at the invaluable Camden Local Studies and Archives Centre at Holborn Library. And a shout out too to the Camden History Society and particularly its 'Streets of...' series of publications, which is such an asset for all who enjoy walking the highways and byways of this city.

Five Leaves Publications
14a Long Row, Nottingham NG1 2DH
www.fiveleaves.co.uk
www.fiveleavesbookshop.co.uk

www.curiouslondon.net

Text © Andrew Whitehead 2018

The moral rights of the author have been asserted

First published 2018

ISBN: 978-1-910170-56-4

Printed and bound in Great Britain